Expelled From The Classroom To

Billionaire
Boardroom

The story of Joseph Valente's rise from
obscurity to hugely successful Managing
Director and winner of The BBC Apprentice

Contents

Hi.

Thanks so Much For buying the book.

If the book is as awesome as you hoped.

Please go to amazon and leave a positive review and share the love for me!

If you do that for me, I'm going to give you something special to say thanks…..

2 free tickets to my one day Event called #MondayMotivation its all things Business & all things Motivation in 2018.

1 month's free subscription to the JosephValenteAcademy that I spoke of in the book, Launching Jan 2018.

Once you've left the review, go to my website www. josephValente.com/Academy

All we need is your Name & Email, with this special code #BestBookEver01

We will then reconcile your name with your review on amazon, get straight in touch & send you the goodies.

I cant wait to meet you all.

Joseph Valente

Author/Entreprenuer/Speaker/TvStar

Foreword

In life there are talkers and doers.

Joseph excels at both. Oh and you can add a 3rd to that list. Writing.

This book really is a wonderfully honest insight into the highs of success and the lows of failure. A story of learning from our experience and bouncing back from those situations when it really doesn't go our way. Welcome to self employment!

That's just how it is. Ultimately your success or failure in life is determined by our ability to make decisions, good and bad.

You want more success? Make better decisions.

The decision to read this book is a good one, and will assist you along the way with your entrepreneurial journey.

Josephs' at times, almost misguided self-belief has served him well, and - as I teach - the first person you have to convince of your brilliance is you!

The second in his case was Sugar.

To win the Apprentice is far from an easy task. You need all manner of business, leadership and persuasion skills, and a massive ladle of charisma during your screen time.

That's a big ask for anyone, let alone someone who was at the time of the show just 25 years old. The run up to the show is hardcore, with 1000s applying; then for the 'lucky' 12 who actually make the show, then run a weekly task gauntlet intended at times to make them look silly.

Imagine having just 15 minutes to do something that should take a seasoned pro a couple of hours.

Welcome to The Apprentice.

The show creates high pressure tasks, to stress test each of the candidates leadership ability in un-winnable situations for the entertainment of the masses.

Over the years, at various business shows across the UK I've spoke on the lineups, with many of those who have been through the gruelling Apprentice process and fallen along the way.

They each tell me (off the record) that the production team set nigh on impossible tasks, putting intentional banana skins in the paths of each of candidates. It's fair to say anyone who watched Josephs' winning season on BBC One would have witnessed it.

That's part of the process, It makes for good telly.

It's how you handle yourself when your play doesn't go your way, that counts.

To win the Apprentice you need to be a whole lot more, than just prime time reality TV entertainment.

You have to have a real vision twinned with a winning business idea.

Joseph has a similar back story to myself. He has street smarts twinned with those ideas, vision and that unwavering self belief and I see so much of my younger self within him.

I was 31 when I started my first business. Joseph 22. Twenty two!

Many people saw his youth as a weakness, stating he was too young to be credible. Maybe his business naivety helped him along the way, he never got the memo that stated he couldn't do it.

It's only a daft idea if it doesn't work. In Josephs' case, ImpraGas did, proving all the doubters wrong.

Over the course of this book you'll learn the reality of what it's like to start a business, the hopes, dreams and having to override those fears that any entrepreneur has, whether they openly prepared to admit it or not.

Twin that with with an intriguing look at life behind the scenes, and the real story of what happened with that boardroom once the TV cameras were turned off...

You are in for a hell of a rollercoaster ride.

Welcome to being an entrepreneur!

Brad Burton
www.BradBurton.biz

4Networking founder
The UK's #1 Motivational Business Speaker

1. Defining Moments

Why did you open up the pages of this book and start reading it right now?

Is it because you've got a passion for business and, like me, are always seeking motivation for the next success?

Is it because you're young, maybe only just leaving school, and you've found yourself at a challenging stage in your life?

Is it because you're a fan of the hit BBC TV show, The Apprentice, and purely want to find out more about what *really* went on - in *and* out of that boardroom - when I won the show back in 2015?

Whatever your motivation, I hope this book is as informative, influential and inspirational for you to read, as it was enjoyable for me to recall, re-live and recount.

***

If I was talking to you now through one of my keynote speeches at a show or event, I'd tell you that I'm about to take you on a journey; thirteen years back to when I had one of those defining moments in life where I vowed that I would never be a victim of my own circumstances.

I was 15, and I was at school. Sadly, I wasn't sitting in a classroom, studiously making notes, or enthusiastically raising my hand to volunteer an answer to a question set by my teacher. Instead, I was sitting between the proverbial rock and a hard place; the rock being my old Head Teacher, and the hard place being the sheer look of disappointment and shame on my mum's face, as she listened in pain to the news that the last straw had been and gone, and that her boy was being kicked out of school.

I won't go into the details of that whole scenario right now, as that's for you to read - should you wish - later in the book. However, what I *will* say is that the look of heartbreak on my mum's face that day, and the tears streaming down from her eyes, gave me all the information I needed to show me that something in my life would need to change. That 15 year-old kid being excluded from school and causing my mum to look at me in shame, or worse, not look at me at all... it shouldn't have been who I was. It was a defining moment.

In hearing words to the effect of the fact that I'd failed her, I attempted to offer my mum the only reassurance that I could; the reassurance that I fully believed in:

Mum, if it's the last thing I do, I will make you proud of me again, one day.

Today, I truly hope the fact that I've worked my way up to a platform where I've been able to write this book and share my whole story in a public forum, is just one way of showing my mum that I meant every word of that promise.

***

Those who follow me on social media will know that I'm quite active when it comes to sharing motivational phrases and inspirational quotes. You don't have to live your life by them, but sometimes they can just give you that much-needed boost or a quick opportunity to reframe your thinking when things are getting you down. If I was to coin or utilise my own go-to quote at this stage in my life, it would be to remind people that you can't buy back time. I personally feel that I took time away from my mum all those years ago, partly due to the natural joy and pain of her taking on parenthood, but mainly due to the fact that my actions as a teenager caused her hours of needless grief and no doubt plenty of sleepless nights. I can't give my mum that time back, but I can do everything I can right now to make sure that any future time she has is purely for her. I really want to pay my mum back, and that's my next promise to her.

Does all of this mean that as long as my mum reads this book I'll have set out to do what I aimed for in writing it? Of course it doesn't. I didn't write this book purely for my mum, although it will become clear that she was a key motivator in how I got to this platform in the first place. Instead, I wanted this book – my story – to be a resource that could inspire generations of business people to get themselves set on the right path to get out there and make a positive difference for their loved ones or even just for themselves - be that in business or in vocation. Maybe some of those people are as young as school-leaving age, and have found themselves in the same position I was in 13 years ago. Maybe they just need a bit of inspiration and guidance at this 'start-up' time in their lives. I'd be delighted if my story could help anyone, really.

Having said all this, I'm not going to rule out a readership here. I don't know whose hands the copy of the book you have in front of you right now have fallen into, but it's my hope that anybody who has a thirst for business or a passion for entrepreneurship, regardless of age, would find something in these pages that will resonate with them. You can't put an age on being motivated or inspired, and it's never too late to go out and act on something that you want or need, so if this book is part of that motivation or inspiration for somebody out there reading it, that's great!

Maybe if you're reading this book it will reaffirm some of your own beliefs. Maybe it will give you a much-needed boost of confidence. Maybe it will spark a controversial topic of discussion. I don't know, but what I *am* certain of is the fact that the book aims to generate some kind of emotion or reaction that will help you to make sure you're on the right journey, and at the right time, for you and your vocation.

I want my book to be an inspiration, as I believe all books should indeed seek to be, because inspiration is key in any walk of life. Having been that 15 year-old kid growing up in Peterborough in the early noughties, with an alcoholic father, a mother who worked three jobs to support us, and my own failed shot at completing a much-needed high school education, I know what it can be like to think at points that there's nobody out there to inspire you, to guide you, and to show you what's possible in life for someone just like you. As you'll read in this book, I was fortunate that I *did* find those sources, but they certainly weren't always readily available to me on a physical or emotional level, and, in one case, I'd never actually met the person I perhaps looked up to the most. Our best sources of motivation can often stem from the most unlikely of places. I truly hope that this book can be one such source for someone out there who really needs it right now.

There is no doubt in my mind that there will be cynics out there who won't be reading this book at any point soon because of two key factors: One, I'm only in my twenties, which is admittedly a little early in life to be writing an autobiography. Two, people will make the assumption that I 'got where I am' purely thanks to the input of Lord Sugar, as a result of me winning the 11th series of the BBC hit TV show, The Apprentice, back in 2015. Both of these viewpoints carry weight, and I don't shy away from that. What I will put forward in response, however, is the fact that firstly, I don't primarily view or want to market this book solely as an 'autobiography' and would rather instead put it out there as a business book, thus making my young age fairly important in this case rather than something to dismiss. Secondly, I stand by the fact that prior to being crowned as the winner of The Apprentice two years ago, I'd already done so much in my previous life to give a significant amount of credibility to what I was already doing and how I was doing it. I may have been a plumber by trade, but I was a business person by heart. I love business, and that's what I'd always wanted to excel in – with or without anyone else's support.

Be open-minded to this book; I don't want it to rest purely as a journey of my own – I want it to be a starting point, or at the very least an inviting fork in the road, to a journey that I hope other people will take themselves. As a result, I'd truly hate it if anyone reading this book, or hearing about its release, thought I was being cocky or arrogant about what I've done in life or in business. I appreciate that I'm only 28 and that my life's journey is nowhere near over. I just personally believe that I have achieved a decent amount by this time and that it's worth me putting it out there into a domain of my peers. I don't want to come across like I'm preaching to people about how to run a business or how to be successful. I just want to see if my story can inspire anyone at all to make either or both of those things happen for them. If it can do these things then that's mission accomplished for me, because my story is about taking risks, leaping into the unknown, handling yourself in tough situations (like a boardroom), and learning how to really put yourself 'out there' in a positive way. Incidentally, the billionaire boardroom experience was not something I either loved or would advise you to get into, but nonetheless, it was something that taught me a lot.

I'm under no illusions that there will be a strong readership out there who can't wait to turn the pages of this book purely due to the fact that they're fans of The Apprentice, where I gained my public recognition by winning back in 2015. If you're one of those people, then I can promise you that this book will not disappoint. I am very fortunate that I now find myself in a position to give fans of the show a true insight into the process, the people and the politics behind what you see on TV and what goes on in real life. I believe I'm the first former Apprentice candidate, and certainly the first winner, to write a book of this type. For the enjoyment of the show's loyal fans, I hope I'm not the last.

I'll be settling down like millions of others to watch the new series of The Apprentice this year, and I'll be hoping to see someone thoroughly deserving of the input and exposure go on to win it. Releasing the book at the same time as the new series of the show where I made a hopefully positive name for myself just feels right. Again, I know I'm young and that people will be cynical, but this really does feel like the right time for me. If I had waited another 13 years to write this book, there would simply be too much to pack in between the covers, as I truly believe that this point right now is nowhere near the end of my success, my journey, or my impact.

When I look back at everything that's happened to me in life, not just during the last thirteen years, but from the last twenty eight in total, I admit that not everything has gone the way I would have wanted it to or even expected it to, but what I *do* know is that my journey is an example of what can be achieved through setting a vision, applying a passion and, to put it bluntly, working your arse off. Although I love that I made my name from plumbing, I don't want to be known solely as 'Joe the Plumber'. I don't believe any of us are necessarily pre-destined for a vocation, and I never believe that anybody's job should define them. Plumbing has most certainly been instrumental in where I've got to today & what has really driven me here is my love for business and being able to turn what I've learnt in this industry into a business. Creating my own venture, in the form of ImpraGas, was always going to be my aim and labour of love since starting up in plumbing, but the challenge *now* is to see where I get ImpraGas to next alongside what else is in store in my journey.

I'm a young person, a businessman, and a guy who wants to do something special with my life. I want people to remember my name. I don't want to waste my time here – I've already talked about how you can't buy that time back. I want to give something back to anyone who might need it, and to show them what's achievable. In the truest sense of 'giving back', I'll be donating copies of this book to colleges within the East Anglia region who offer apprenticeships within the industry where I started to build my success. I don't have my own kids at the moment, so in the meantime, if I can help other kids out there with something that may benefit them, then that sounds like a great next step in my journey to me.

You could argue either before or after reading my book that what I've achieved in my life isn't overly impressive. This wholeheartedly depends on what you use as your measure of success. My own personal measure is that for a 28 year-old who refused to be a victim of his own circumstances, I've certainly done alright.

I started off this chapter, and this book, by talking about my belief that we all have at least one defining moment in life. These moments can take any form, and they can come at any time. Defining moments are those that can stop you from falling, shove you down some unfamiliar pathway, or completely turn you around. This book documents each of the defining moments in my own life, so I'll take you back to where it all began.

2. A Four Year Old's Mentality

When you're trying to understand life at the age of four, you construct a mental model of how things should 'be', and you base this on the things you are used to; the clothes people wear, they toys kids play with, and the places you go to get or experience these things. With my own four year-old mentality, things were happening in my life that made me start to see that things were different for different people. I was beginning to compare, and I was beginning to question.

I wanted *everything*, as most kids do, and if I didn't get things when I asked for them, then I would question *why*. I wasn't so much questioning why I didn't or couldn't have them, but questioning why other people *could*. I need to point out that I wasn't a brat and I certainly wasn't spoilt; illustrated perfectly by the fact that I hardly ever got what I asked for! However, I was a typical kid in terms of poring over catalogues and drawing circles around the toys that I wanted. I recognised that some of the circled items had a large price tag attached to them, but I still didn't connect with why I couldn't have them.

My mum worked a lot, so why did she always tell me I'd have to "*wait until Christmas*"? Mum worked three or four jobs simultaneously throughout most of my young life. She was a dinner lady at a local school, and then stayed on to work in the afterschool club. She would then get on her bike each night to get across to local people's houses to clean for them. After a busy working week, she would then get up early on a Saturday morning to go and clean at the local bakery.

My dad was the polar opposite. I never once recalled him having a job. What he truly skilled at, though, was spending my mum's wages. Everything she earned, he had a solid go at cleaning out; mainly by spending it on excessive amounts of alcohol and cigarettes. Us kids were always mum's priority, though, and while we certainly never had the absolute best of everything, she always made sure that my older sister (Chiara) and I never went without. I may never have had a new bike, but a second-hand bike was still a bike. Chiara and I never missed out on school trips because mum would make sure that the money was there to see that we could have the same opportunities as the rest of our classmates. All good parents do these things for their kids, but I look back now and see that this will have been significantly harder for my mum, who was essentially supporting two kids and a waste of space husband, whilst working four jobs and single-handedly running a house. I never remember her buying anything for herself. Her thoughts were always of her kids, and in keeping our house – our home – running.

Though there was nothing really 'there' in terms of any kind of relationship with my dad, he did play a significant role in my life, in some respect. My dad was an inconvenience to me, right up until the point when he left the family home when I was 13. There was no love lost in either direction, and I honestly didn't see the point in him being around, so I wasn't surprised or bothered when he left. I don't know if as the years have gone on my mind has been clouded with sour adult judgements, but I honestly can't think of anything good to say about him. I should have respected my dad even if I didn't like him, but there was nothing to respect. Respect is the key to all good relationships, and I didn't have any for my dad because there was simply nothing I liked, appreciated or admired about him. Instead, the male influence that filled that role was my mum's older brother – my Uncle Tim. We didn't get to see him often, but whenever he visited, he really made an impact.

The first thing I think of when I remember Uncle Tim - from my four year-old's perspective - was that he was tall. This of course sounds ridiculous because I was four years old, so *all* adults were tall. He seemed taller than most men I'd seen or met, however. I have no idea if this is because he just was indeed a lofty man, or because he appeared this way because of how he presented himself; head held high, walking with purpose, and all of this crowned by an impressive shock of white hair. He had this kind of aura around him. He had presence.

I loved it when Uncle Tim visited. He would always bring gifts for me and for my sister, and he would always have something that my mum could use for the house, like a TV or some electrical bit of kit. I remember that he always had some piece of tech with him, and this would be most notable when he'd turn up at school assemblies and film the whole thing. He'd always take us out to eat, or buy in a takeaway when he visited, and this was a big deal at the time, as we saw those things as a luxury. On Christmas Day each year, Uncle Tim would turn up at my nan's house and the whole place would be transformed into a sea of presents. Christmastime was also extra special with Uncle Tim because we'd always have a day out somewhere, and I just loved spending time in his company; watching him, idolising him, learning from him. I remember him really making me laugh on one trip out, where I think we were at Warwick Castle. He put on an obviously fake Swedish accent at the entrance gate in order to blag getting in on a tourist discount... and no, I've never tried this myself.

Although he always loved to blag, and did so with a charm that I so wanted to emulate as I grew up, my Uncle Tim was a hard worker. He was Managing Director of a big car finance company, and over the years he had worked his way up from the bottom to the top. He wore smart suits and drove great cars. He's a very private man so I won't say too much more about him, but I have to mention that nobody ever seemed to say 'no' to him. I don't like the word 'no', and even as a small child I had a real problem with the word. Please don't get me wrong, because I wasn't a brat who kicked off every time he was told 'no' - which I heard a *lot* and for many reasons - but it was a word that annoyed me when it related to why we couldn't have something based on the fact that we couldn't afford it. I began to realise over the years that whilst I loved everything Uncle Tim did for us, there was something wrong with how our family were living. I'd said earlier how my dad was significant, and it was because his existence allowed me to form a comparison in my mind. My dad should have been doing all the things that Uncle Tim was doing; giving the gifts he was giving and spending the time he was spending. If Uncle Tim could have great things, why couldn't we get them without him having to provide it all for us? I learned in time that Uncle Tim was simply a harder worker and in a higher paid job with a better career than my dad; which admittedly wasn't hard. Uncle Tim wasn't born like that, however; he went out and earned it.

I wanted to be like my Uncle Tim in the sense that I wanted to be the person who looked after my mum. I wanted to surprise her and to provide her with things that she may want or need. That was always important to me, and it will always be my long-term goal. Much as I appreciated Uncle Tim and was grateful for everything he gave and did, I never wanted my family to have someone else providing for us. One day, that would be my job.

I was seven years old when I began to get my first taste of success to set me on that road to follow in

Uncle Tim's footsteps. It was 1996, and I had seemingly developed the skills and ability to hustle, sell and make money. I understood the basics of what making money was all about, and I'd found a way to do this from something I loved. If you were a football nut growing up in the nineties, you were no doubt into the craze of collecting football stickers, and you'll be more than familiar with the Merlin Sticker Books. If this doesn't ring a bell, then allow me to elaborate. Merlin produced small packs of football stickers that you could buy in almost any newsagent's, corner shop or supermarket. You got six stickers in each sealed pack for around 27p, and each sticker documented a squad player from the Premier League. Once in a blue moon, you'd tear open the packet and strike gold (or rather silver), seeing that you'd obtained a 'shiny' - a somewhat sparkly version of a sticker depicting one of the 20 Premiership Club badges. Because they were so rare, everybody wanted a shiny. The opposite rule applied the other way around, where in the case of the least common squad players from perhaps the lower ranking teams, you'd end up with several copies of that player's sticker. It was a lottery, and that's what added to the excitement and intrigue of the purchase.

Collecting the stickers was one hobby, but pasting them into an official Merlin sticker album was another entirely. The album was a place for you to take pride in your work and to more closely analyse your stock. They sold for around £2 or £3. The people at Merlin were clever, and knew that the more elusive they made the shiny stickers and the stickers for the higher profile players, the more packs people would buy in order to attempt to rectify the situation. They'd created a market.

My family didn't have a great deal of money when I was growing up, as I've already alluded to, and getting hold of 27p each time I felt the craving for Merlin stickers was tough. What I *did* find I was often in possession of, however, was a stack of duplicate stickers obtained from the times when I was indeed fortunate to stock up from the shop. There was no sense in keeping these duplicates, and the best way to offload them was to trade them for stickers that you *did* need, in return for the other person gaining one from your collection that they in turn desired. This process was known as 'swapsies', and I'm fairly sure you'll have heard of that concept. I'd always go to the 'older side' of the playground when conducting swapsies, because dealing with the kids my own age was a waste of time. Like me, they just didn't have enough money to have accrued a big enough stock of stickers. Somehow, I had earned a certain level of respect from the older kids, who were say ten or eleven years old, which ultimately allowed me to do deals with them. I was sharp, smart, and had an eye for a deal, meaning I'd nearly always leave their side with a fresh deck of stickers to put in my album.

My business model ran beautifully for a while, but eventually began to fizzle. Merlin were flooding the packets with the same old lower profile players that nobody really wanted or needed, and so everyone's available swapsies became the same. I began thinking that I'd really need money to buy fresh packs, but I could only manage this if I was able to get money for my existing stickers rather than swapping them in trades. So, one night I sat on the living room floor and gathered together all my eligible swapsies. I started to pile them all into random stacks of 10. Occasionally, I would make a stack of 11. Those particular stacks carried a twist, or rather, they carried a shiny, and the way I would market those stacks would be to guarantee the presence of that shiny to potential buyers. I knew from my own drive to buy that other kids like me would pay a premium (if they had it) to definitely get their hands on something they knew they needed.

Chiara sat with me later that night and together we cut pieces of old-style computer paper – the stuff with the run of holes down either side - into small square sections. We then slotted the stacks of stickers in between sections of the paper, stapled them shut around the sides, and wrote "VALENTE FOOTBALL STICKERS 25p" across the front of each package. What I had created, aged 7, were my own football sticker packs to rival Merlin. Although the packs were rustic in presentation, I knew they would prove attractive to my market; coming in at 2p less than the Merlin packs, and promising at least four additional stickers per pack. Essentially, these were the same stickers that I couldn't shift for free in a swapsies deal, but it seemed that people would indeed pay money to take a gamble on the possibility of gaining something they really wanted or needed. All it took the next day was for the first kid to bite at the deal, and when he did so, selecting an 11-pack containing a 'shiny' in the process, I soon had a frenzy on my hands for my Valente Football Stickers. All of my packs were gone before the sounding of the end of the break-time bell, and I'd made **£3.50 in those fifteen minutes.** Those ten and twenty pence pieces were burning a hole in my pocket, and I couldn't wait for school to finish so that I could get myself down to the shop to buy up as many Merlin packs as I could with the profits, in the hope that it would take me much closer to completing my sticker album.

My Merlin album may not have filled up that day, but my head was most certainly filled with ideas. I now had proof that I could make something out of nothing, and believed that if I wanted something enough, I could always find a way to go about getting it. I kept the marketing going for a while, and though it guaranteed me money, it wasn't about that. The biggest success was the sense of achievement I ultimately got from completing my Merlin sticker album. You should always have an end goal. When you complete that, you should set another one. For me, I branched out into 'Pogs' and 'Tazos', before eventually running my own 'buy for 5p, sell for 10p' tuck shop business. I was moving on up, and primary school was as good a place as any for a kid from Peterborough to do it.

Though you already know what's coming in terms of my actual education whilst at school – getting expelled at the age of 15 etc – you may not believe it but I was actually a really good kid at primary level; and a clever one, too. I was top of the class in literally all subjects, and I had a thirst for each and every one of them. It's always been my mission to learn in every area of life and business in order to have a sound knowledge of the basics. Once you have those, you can go on to specialise in the areas that you really love and excel at. Primary school is that perfect place to learn those basics in education, and I thrived there. I particularly loved maths, and was always trying to reach the higher level of work to that which was initially set to me. Writing was also something I loved, and Science held an immense amount of intrigue for me, also. I was creative in subjects like Art and I had the energy and natural talent that helped me excel in PE and school sport. I really was an all-rounder, as teachers say, and as well as always being the first with my hand up in class, I was often top of that class in my grades, too. I relished homework, believe that or not, and I loved continuing my learning outside of school and structured lessons. I even went for the top roles in all the school plays and put myself forward for key parts in school assemblies. My ambition wasn't to be clever as such, but to be the absolute best and the biggest achiever out of everybody.

Having said all of this, I had a mischievous and rebellious side, too. I would always be up to something cheeky, even if it was relentlessly peevish. For example, if the school dinner ladies said we weren't allowed on the school field at break-time after it had been raining,

I would go and stand on it anyway. It wasn't so much about rebellion, but about having control over instances where people were saying 'no' to me.

My attitude at home in terms of my mischievous streak was a hell of a lot worse, what without having the joy of learning to keep me on track. I was never in the house and was always out playing everywhere I could and missing every curfew. To say I pushed boundaries and my own luck was an understatement. If mum told me I could only go so far on my bike, I'd go one street further, just to say that I could. Whatever she told me I couldn't do, even if it was because it was something stupidly dangerous, I'd do it anyway, just to prove a point. In addition to that, I would then go home and openly tell my mum that I'd done it. It was as if I wanted to prove that whatever it was I was told I couldn't or shouldn't do, I had survived having done it. The word 'no' became my challenge. If mum hadn't have mentioned things at all, I probably wouldn't have even felt compelled or remotely interested in doing them, but that foreboding that I couldn't do something was almost like a dare. No response my mum could have given as to why I couldn't go somewhere or do something would have kept me safe. I even rode a motorbike when I was about 12 years old. The thrill wasn't so much the action, but the satisfaction I'd get after the event from announcing that I'd done it.

Even when I was at my tamest, I loved being out. Whether it was the playground, park or street, I was always involved with something, and my true passion was hustling other kids and doing deals, thanks to the success of my Valente Football Stickers venture. I'd always forget my pen at school and so would constantly borrow them from other kids. This quickly extended to rulers and rubbers etc, and I soon realised I'd built my own stationery empire! If I needed or wanted something then I'd figure out a way to get it – a trade, a deal or a blag. I just loved the process. I may still have had little in the way of money, but I'd learned quickly that when money couldn't get you something, you could use skill and persuasion as currency.

Even my own sister, Chiara, wasn't exempt from my actions. She was three years older than me and saw me very much as her annoying little brother. What made the divide worse is that she was a girly girl in her pursuits, and I was more a stereotypical boisterous boy at the time. Every game we attempted to play together ended up in an argument, and it was usually my fault because I liked to cheat. Monopoly was always a disaster in our house, with Chiara getting increasingly frustrated with the fact that I would always be taking sly notes from the bank when she wasn't looking. I was literally robbing the bank. We did have some similarities though, as we were both very focused and understood that earning money and work were important in life; an ethic clearly instilled in us by our mum. By the time she was 14, Chiara had got herself a job, and though I still annoyed her, she would often give me some of her earnings to spend, even if it was just 50p or so. A lot of the time when she couldn't be bothered going to the shops, she'd give me the money to go and get stuff for her on her behalf. I would never agree to do this without some kind of compensation, however, and would always negotiate a fee for carrying out the task. She thought this was irritating, but I thought it was enterprising. I walked Chiara down the aisle at her wedding last year, and gave what is usually the traditional Father of the Bride speech. It was one of the proudest moments of my life.

What did I learn from everything in this stage of my early life? I learned that there are always ways and means when you're presented with a 'no'. I learned that there are always options to get things you don't have. I learned that the best way to capitalise on any situation is to think about what you have - not what you *don't* have. My philosophy from this became the mantra of *create, maintain and continue to grow*, but we'll look more at that in a later chapter...

3. Expelled From The Classroom

So, you already know what's coming in this chapter, but hear me out in finding out how I found myself being expelled from high school. Believe me, I'm not proud of it.

As adolescence kicked in around the start of secondary school, my inability to accept the word 'no' formed a toxic mix with my general attitude that I did not, under any circumstances, like being told what to do. I would mess around, play up and kick off in any lesson that I didn't want to be in. Funnily enough, this wasn't because I didn't want to *learn*, but because I didn't want to learn in that particular subject I ended up disrupting. If it didn't interest me, and I already knew the basics, then I didn't see the point. I would literally rather have gone for an extra Maths session than sit through something like Art during this time in my life. As an adult, I completely understand that for many reasons, classroom education needs to broadly offer a 'one size fits all' approach, but this is not going to work for a lot of kids, and it certainly didn't work for me. My education became a dirge of repetition rather than the thing of joy it had been at primary level.

Secondary school was all about grades and exams, and I knew I wasn't 'up to' the grades required to do well in a variety of those assessments, so I didn't see the point in trying. When you get older, you apply for jobs that you're good at, and you don't enter into that arena with the aim of taking on every role within that company or business. For example, you wouldn't find an engineer looking to excel or even participate in admin or sales. In my own company, Impragas, I'm not going to turn away a perfectly good engineer because they fail to make a sale – it's not their skill set. To me, school felt like you were expected to be good at *everything*, and this is never going to be possible at a high level for most people, so why grade or judge them on it all and waste their time?

I was emerging at school and at home as the kind of lad who wanted to be the 'Alpha' – the top dog. My dad had wanted to fulfil this role at home and thought he could do this by shouting and being controlling, but he had nothing to back this up. I knew that in order to truly lead, I'd need something about me. To assert this stance at home with my dad, it was very much like the young lion wanting to grow up to take out the older lion. This felt like natural instinct for me at home, so as I got older, I began challenging my dad whenever I could. I couldn't be told at home and I wouldn't be told at school, and the arguments I faced at the former set me up in a negative way for the latter. I was completely in the wrong mindset by the time I arrived at the school gates at 8.50am each morning. Teachers will never fully know what's going on with their kids internally, and I don't envy that part of their job at all. There's an argument there that teachers are not given the time, training or resource to dig to this depth, but whatever the reason, because I couldn't connect with my teachers, I learned to lose respect for *all* authority, and as a consequence, the teachers took the brunt of my resentment as the people I saw most each day. I was 12, I was vile, and I didn't care.

By the time I was 13, dad had moved out of our house. By the time I was 14, I was hanging around with much older kids who quite possibly weren't the best influence on me, even though it was my choice to be with them. I don't know why those kids welcomed me into their group, with me being a good three or four years younger than them, but they seemed to like my rebellion and my spark. I was cocky and I thought I knew everything, but don't all teenagers? I guess I zoned in on an older group because I wanted to someone to look up to and someone to give me respect in return.

My own personal circumstances and personality amplified the natural rebellion of being a teenager. I was labelled left, right and centre, and I wanted to live up to the claims and down to the expectations. I wanted to prove people right whenever they thought badly of me. Having said all of this, deep down I knew this was a temporary phase. I may have looked like a lost cause to so many people, but in my own eyes, I had belief that I would go on to do something great – eventually.

The one label that was thrown around as a relentless warning was the fact that I would eventually end up expelled. In my head, I thought "*fine, let's do this*", until I did indeed get expelled, and I've alluded already to the jolt that this gave me. Obviously, there were many things that led up to that situation before it happened. For example, I would do anything I could to get out of going to what I considered to be boring lessons. I'd get the wrong bus to school or get off at the wrong stop just to waste time. I'd turn up in trainers knowing that I'd be sent out or sent home. I wanted a reaction at each turn, and to cause inconvenience to the running of the day.

In secondary school, as I've mentioned, I wanted to develop a few subject areas, but certainly not all. Technology was a good one for me because it was practical and I got to use my imagination to create things. As a primary school kid I'd always liked the creativity of Art lessons, too. As a secondary school kid however, it was a different story. I really couldn't do it. It was less about the creativity and more about the technical ability at that stage, and there was no enjoyment in that for me. I didn't see the point. Plus, I also don't understand how the education system can justify the 'grading' of a predominantly creative subject. My poor grades and the inability I had to fulfil the briefs – mainly through drawing – just really put me off. For me, Art is a talent that you either have or you don't. It's not like Science, where I personally believe you can actually learn the facts and get better at understanding and applying them if you have the patience over time. I liked Science, but it seemed that even that subject wasn't a foolproof way of engaging me. In one lesson, I deliberately set a pot of magnesium on fire, after I'd heard the teacher reference the Catherine Wheel-like effects that such a reaction would spark. You can picture the outcomes, I'm sure.

In the playground, if I wasn't doing my deals, I was getting into scuffles with other kids. I actually had no issues with any of my peers so I don't know why I ever did that. Whatever the reason, I was dragging them down with me. In some ways I was an outcast, but in other ways I found I could be part of everything, but either way, I never committed to tying myself to one particular group. Generally though, I was a distraction to others. I made it impossible for teachers to teach, and I was stopping kids from learning. I wasn't learning anything myself, anyway.

The end point all came about a few months before I turned 15, when my school reached breaking point with my behaviour. Looking back, they had done an immense amount of work to attempt to get me on track and keep me in education, and I never appreciated or even acknowledged any of it. Eventually, they launched a last ditch attempt to 'save' me. It was actually a fantastic way out and a great opportunity for a young teenager, but naturally, I didn't care about this or even recognise it at the time. All of my teachers agreed that I wasn't learning, and I know for certain they will have felt that me being in school was just no use to anyone at best, and a disruption to others at worst. They had formed a plan with Peterborough Regional College, and they would be sending me for one day per week to engage on a vocational taster course in Plumbing. I had never thought about plumbing before, but the college had just introduced the course, and my school were out of any other options. I was being sent along to the college course with Nathan, who was pretty much my best friend at the time, and was also on the same sinking 'risk of expulsion' ship as me. I have no idea why the school thought it was a good idea to keep us together, but as I said, they were out of any other real choices. This was unlikely to end well.

As it turned out, I quite liked the plumbing course. I had the freedom to make my own way there each time as well, and so it was a step in the right direction towards independence. However, I still wasn't taking things as seriously as I should have done, and so one day, Nathan and I caught a different bus together and instead went and spent the day in the Peterborough City Centre. It was only once, but it was enough, and we got caught. I'd lasted three months on the plumbing course, and now it was over, as the college were understandably not happy to put up with that behaviour given the circumstances as to why I was enrolled there in the first place. It was a massive shame for a lot of reasons, and I really do mean it when I say I enjoyed the course and gained something from it. I accept now, however, that my attitude was all wrong, and so it really didn't matter what was going on or given to me at the time – I was never going to succeed.

When I talk to school-age kids these days about their options, I will always tell them this story and about how it is absolutely essential that you have the right attitude and the ability to take responsibility. There will always be times when you just need to do things for yourself, even when others are trying to help you. It seemed that at 15, I just wasn't accepting help, and it was becoming clear that I just needed to be removed from things completely in order to see where I was going and what I needed to do. If the Head Teacher himself would have sat the GCSE exams for me and given me certificates with 'A' grades on them, it still wouldn't have helped me. I needed waking up.

By this time, my mum had a new man in her life and this brought her a new focus – quite deservedly. I was on my own. I was sick of telling myself that there was a reason I behaved the way I did and that there was someone or something else to blame. These things hit me on the afternoon shortly after I'd been caught skiving from college. As well as the Head Teacher, my Head of Year, Mr Tivey, was also in the office to help deliver the news to my mum and I that I was about to be expelled. I've already said how I was gutted for my mum, but I was also gutted for Mr Tivey. He had always bent over backwards to try to help me throughout my time at school, and for some reason, he always believed in me. I'd really let him down and I couldn't look him in the eye. I'd thrown everything he'd ever done for me back in his face. I didn't lay eyes Mr Tivey again until ten years later, when I saw him on TV. He was interviewed as part of the 'Final Five' episode of The Apprentice, and just as he had been back in high school, he was full of praise for me, and for the person he'd apparently been watching me go on to become. I can't believe that after everything I'd put him through, he did that for me on camera. I will never forget that, and I'll never be able to thank him enough.

It sounds strange, but I was lucky that I got expelled. It was the right thing to happen for everyone. It was time to start proving people *wrong* instead of right, and carrying myself down a more positive path. Firstly, however, there was one more hurdle to face. I was sent to what is now known as a Pupil Referral Unit, or a PRU. A PRU is a place where excluded children are sent in the hope that they can be educated, engaged or positively distracted enough to save them from ending up as a 'NEET' statistic – 'Not in Education, Employment or Training'. I can't comment as to generally how well such places worked back then or even work now, but from my perspective at the time, I was thrown in with all the other 'bad kids' from the area, and it was understandably not a good mix! Being badly behaved (to put it mildly) was a badge of honour, and there was a hierarchy as to who was the worst. A lot of the kids in there made me look angelic, but however I viewed it, that place was not a good environment for me to be in. I wanted a way out, so one day, I just never went back. They never came calling or looking for me... believe me, they had bigger worries to contend with.

Schools have changed a lot in the last ten or fifteen years and now provide many alternatives to pure academic pathways for their students. Vocational courses are key, although I still don't think these options are talked about enough or presented in the light that they should be. In other words, vocational subjects are often seen or talked about as 'drop out' subjects; the ones you *have* to choose because you can't achieve academically in line with whatever present standards are being heralded at the time. It shouldn't be like this. Vocational subjects should be seen as a mindset option or a choice, and schools should be key in promoting this and have access to figureheads and role models who have followed such pathways and been successful. I recently went back to my old high school to speak to the Year 10s and 11s, and much as I was delighted to talk of success stories to the kids wanting to look at vocational study, I was even more pleased that the new Head Teacher was so keen to point out everything that the school was already doing to promote such routes in education. He was really big on construction in general, and took so much pleasure in showing me all of the projects that the school was currently involved in for that field.

Although I threw my own vocational (plumbing) option away at school, I often wonder that if the course I got sent on had been introduced to me at a younger age, as I believe such things *should* be in schools, then it would have 'hooked' me early enough and I wouldn't have found myself jumping out of a course that I actually quite liked. On the other hand, maybe I wouldn't also be where I am today, but I'd like to think those paths would have merged eventually. For me, when it comes to any intervention or options for kids, the sooner they're presented the better.

There are so many messages I still to this day take from my whole high school experience. I hope that I can pass these on to anyone who may need these, so what I focus on is this: Looking back, my actions will always have had casualties. I didn't *want* to drag anyone else down with me, but that will most certainly have happened anyway. I felt for the school because I know now that they really couldn't just 'get rid' of me. If you are in business, though, you have choice. It goes without saying that I would never advocate getting rid of a member of staff instantaneously the minute there are problems. Just as the school had proved with me, you as a manager, supervisor or leader have a pastoral duty to at least try to work with the person concerned to sort things out. Take advice, look for different pathways, reach out and engage. However, if the behaviour continues and those people you are dealing with are unresponsive to your efforts, you need to get rid. You cannot let them disrupt what you're doing and distract from what you are trying to achieve, because they'll take down everything, and most likely, every*one* in the process. School should have kicked me out sooner, but they had to keep me because it's the law, I guess. In business though, a person should want to be there at your job, so there really are few excuses for someone causing issues for your staff, your project or your brand. Do what you need to do, and remember, the sooner the better.

4. Lucky Number Seven

15 years old, and seemingly nothing to be proud of or to aim for.

Mum had pretty much given up on me by this time, and the police were starting to take a slight interest in me thanks to my - albeit low-level - rebellious behaviour. I was not in a good place.

In low profile deals on the streets, I was trading mobile phones. My end goal was to work my way up to owning a David Beckham endorsed flip-phone, which at the time would have been retailing for around £500. I think I ended up getting mine for something closer to the £100 mark... I always made sure I got a great deal and enjoyed the process along the way. Computer games were also a favourite of mine to trade. I made sure I enjoyed each one first, though, despite my short attention span. There was always such a buzz for me in swapping and selling, but I'd only do this with computer games once I'd fully completed them. I saw this as my success – complete the game, and then you can sell it. I'd buy and play with any games really, and would see the benefit of having three fairly rubbish computer games if there was hope that I could use them one day to get the latest FIFA or similar. Everything served a purpose.

In terms of *real* purpose, however, I had absolutely nothing to do each day and nowhere to go, so I decided I needed to create an opportunity for myself, seeing as the old adage that this always comes knocking didn't seem to be ringing true. It's a phrase I don't to this day believe in banking on.

I needed to draw on whatever resources I could, so I went out to seek a local plumber I knew fairly well. Darren was the cousin of a friend of mine, and even though he was about ten years older than me, he'd always been a friendly face and a decent guy in his attitude towards me. Darren owned his own plumbing company. He'd done well for himself financially and this showed in the BMW he drove around town. More importantly to me though, Darren had always seemed to be a well-respected lad in our area. For me, Darren appeared to have made it.

I approached Darren, and in my usual honesty, told him what had happened with school and the plumbing course at Peterborough College. I came straight out and asked Darren if I could work for him; for a year, for free. There would have been no reason on earth why Darren – or anybody – would have paid me to work for them given my track record, so I knew that volunteering my time and energy was my best bet if I was to have any hope at all of somebody taking me seriously.

I wasn't just interested in getting myself off the streets, so to speak; I wanted Darren to train me and for me to learn from him. I wanted purpose, and my end goal at this time was that I wanted to train and learn under a professional until the timing was right to enrol on a college course, based on the experience that I had gained within a trade I actually quite liked. Ideally, I wanted Darren to be the one to enrol me onto a college apprenticeship, and for him to be the one who would then pay me to carry out the 'on the job' elements of such a course. I put all this to Darren and told him that I'd only expect him to do this if he thought I was worth it. He liked me, and he liked the proposal, so he agreed to take me on. I went on to work for him, as promised, every single day for a year.

For the first time in my teenage life, I dealt respectfully with authority. I did exactly what I was told and I did it willingly. Perhaps it was because I respected Darren. Perhaps it was because I wanted him to respect me. Perhaps it was because I'd finally learned a life lesson. Whatever the reason, I was a model employee, and this was helped by the fact that it was my choice to be there; working and learning with Darren as a way to occupy my time and my mind. I couldn't get mad or angry at anything if all of this was of my own volition. I needed to be accountable.

I was learning so much from Darren and benefitting every day from the chance he had taken on me. I was grateful. He'd had a similar upbringing to me and had done really well for himself, so I wanted to impress him and I wanted to make him proud. I wanted to show him, and myself, that every day, I was helping him and making a contribution to the work he was doing and business he was building.

Not long after my 16th birthday, when my year with Darren was up, my mentor kept his word. He enrolled me into Peterborough College. I know what you're thinking, and yes - that was indeed the same place I'd been excluded from on the last plumbing course I was on. I can't lie, it was a worry. Either the good people at the college didn't remember me, or my past had been significantly overlooked, but right now, my name was on the enrolment and acceptance forms for a two-year apprenticeship there, centring round an NVQ Level 2 qualification in Plumbing and Heating. My timetable showed the names of tutors I'd never met before, so I counted my blessings that I would definitely be getting the fresh start at that college I'd wanted - if not deserved based on my original time spent there. For the first time in a long while, there was a glimmer of hope in my mum's eyes.

The apprenticeship was going great in terms of both my studies and my work-based learning with Darren. Three months in, however, Darren called me. It was just before Christmas. He reluctantly gave me the news that he was splitting with his business partner and effectively needing to shut down the company. I was mortified for him because I knew how hard he had worked to build that business, but mainly I was devastated for myself because I knew my course couldn't possibly continue now. More importantly, I had thoroughly loved working for Darren, and I couldn't imagine my life right now not being mentored by him. I rang the college the next day to tell them. They were genuinely sympathetic but couldn't do much to help me as, in their words, *"apprenticeship placements are like gold-dust, Joseph"*. They told me that in order to continue my enrolment on the course, I would only have a three week window to find another employer.

I picked up the Yellow Pages for the Peterborough area and called every single plumber, builder and electrician listed. I sent out copies of my CV, and even got myself out locally to knock on the doors of the tradesmen listed within walking distance. With one week to go prior to the college deadline, a local plumber with his own business heard me out. Looking back, I had completely overstated what I could do as an apprentice plumber, but I was desperate to be taken on. The tradesman seemed to like what he heard and agreed to give me a chance. Relief was mine.

Thinking that this was too good to be true, my relief didn't last long, and it became clear within a matter of weeks that this guy was less of a plumber and more of a cowboy builder. He'd taken me on to be his skivvy, and if you think I mean he had me cleaning the plumbing equipment or making cups of tea, you'd be wrong. Everything he had me doing was for his *own* benefit, not for his business. He had me cleaning his car, cutting his grass, and even insulating his loft. I was learning nothing. On top of all this, he was a pretty nasty guy. I remember on one morning, my moped - purchased as a result my various entrepreneurial dealings - had failed to start. I called my boss and he told me he'd pick me up. Little did I know that he was going to dock my £80 per week apprenticeship wage £15 for the privilege of the lift. When the same working day was done, he pulled his van up at his house and left me out on the street whilst he went in for the night. I had no cash, no battery on my phone, and had to walk a mile in the cold just to get to the nearest payphone to make a reverse charge call to see if my mum could pick me up.

Clearly I had little luck with two-wheeled vehicles or bosses, because later that season when the weather turned treacherous, I crashed my newly traded-up motorbike after slipping on some black ice on the route to my boss's house to start work. I was always early for work, but obviously the freak accident set me back on this occasion. When I eventually turned up cold, shocked and bruised at my boss's house and explained what had happened, he looked me dead in the eyes and told me I should have set off earlier. Nice guy, hey?

One morning, when the weather was a little better, my boss appeared in a much sunnier mood. He handed me some thick gloves and a roll of black bin-bags. With a growing smirk he told me that I'd love the project he was sending me to work on and that it would keep me busy for days. He drove me to a flat in a desolate part of the city. It turns out that my boss owned the flat, but rented it to who turned out to be local drug addicts. Basically, the place was a smack den. For whatever reason, the addicts had gone, but every trace of them having been there still remained. The place was trashed, and it was beyond a mess; it was unsafe. There was shit everywhere, and sadly I do mean that literally. There were used needless on almost every surface, and the wax from burning candles soiled the only remaining 'clean' patches of the floor. My boss left, and I must have stood there in that squalor for half an hour, contemplating. I called my mum.

I couldn't think of anywhere in the world I'd want to be any less, but I also didn't want to leave because I'd worked too damn hard to get this 'placement'. I couldn't quit. Okay, I wasn't learning anything at all, and my health, safety and mental well-being were all at serious risk, but what if I couldn't find another plumber to sign off my hours and pay the terms of this apprenticeship qualification I so desperately wanted? Mum told me to get out straight away, and said that if I couldn't listen to her, I'd at least have to call the college to tell them what was going on. Unsurprisingly, my tutor told me to get out with immediate effect. With mixed emotions, I hung up the phone, walked out of the front door, and didn't look back. I never spoke to my employer again, and I don't really care what happened to him. So much had been invested into that apprenticeship, so if college wouldn't have insisted I left, I think I probably would have stayed – I was *that* hungry to get that qualification. I had worked so hard and put up with so much, and right now, I was in tears.

With the three week deadline once again hanging over my head, I was somehow fortunate enough to meet and gain employment with a guy called Shaun. He was a top bloke, and certainly one of the best plumbers I've ever worked with to this day. I learned a lot from him immediately, and I felt really respected by him. He told me he knew I was willing to do anything to work, based on the fact that one day in the first week, during a blizzard, I'd set off two hours early on my motorbike, so that if anything bad happened as with my previous icy encounter, I'd still have a chance of getting to work on time. Frozen half to death when I turned up at their house 90 minutes early, Shaun's wife told me off (with affection) for being so stupid. Shaun himself said the weather was so bad he wasn't even going to risk taking the van out, and he called off our work day entirely.

At the same time as I'd applied for a position with Shaun, I'd applied for another job elsewhere, which is understandable given how much of a struggle this whole apprenticeship was turning out to be on the employment side. Three weeks into my employment with Shaun, the owner of the company I'd applied to had returned from holiday and called me for an interview. I was intrigued and wanted to attend because I knew that the experience of actually having an interview rather than purely pitching my services as a cold caller would benefit me. Straight after the interview, the company in question offered me a job, and even offered me double the going apprenticeship rate. I'm disappointed to say that this element was all I focussed on at that time. Without even thinking about how much I loved working for Shaun and how good he was to me, and how much I was learning under his guidance, I zoned in on the cash incentive and accepted the new offer. Shaun was really understanding of the situation, which in some ways made things worse. I said goodbye to my wonderful mentor, but then realised within weeks of doing so that the grass really isn't always greener, and that money is most certainly not everything...

My tutors at college weren't exactly thrilled with my decision, but they were relieved that the end of my work with Shaun was at least voluntary on this occasion. The way I saw it at the time, was that I was getting the same apprenticeship, but with double the money. Obviously, as an adult, I feel compelled to tell any kids out there reading this that this really isn't always the comparison. You need to look at *all* of the circumstances and weigh up everything that you gain against everything you will need to sacrifice in making such a decision. Put it this way, if this new company would have offered me the same money that Shaun was paying, I'd never have left to join them. Why? Because I liked and respected Shaun as my boss, his knowledge was second to none, and I'd learned more from him in three weeks than most apprentices learn in a year. There was no logical reason to leave Shaun's employment. I will always kick myself for that.

It seemed karma was to pay me back, however, because one month into my role with the new company, I threw it all away. I was due to work early on a Saturday morning, but the Friday night before my shift, being a 17 year old lad, I'd gone out with my mates and got drunk. This isn't anything new for a working teenage lad, but because I was earning twice the money these days, I was feeling like I could *spend* twice the amount, too. Spend I did, to the point where I couldn't hold my alcohol that night and woke up on the Saturday morning with the worst hangover I'd ever had. Rather than getting up and working, or at least calling my boss to (pathetically) ring in sick, I fell back to sleep and slept through the rest of the working day. My boss was understandably livid with me, and fired me on the spot. It was the only job I'd been fired from, and it shocked me to the point where I vowed that it would never ever happen again. After all I'd been through with this apprenticeship through no fault of my own, I'd now taken this aspect in my own hands and well and truly demolished it. I deserved the repercussions.

So, I dug out the Yellow Pages again. I picked up the phone again. I got out on the road again. I was only five months into this two year course, and for whatever reasons, I was now approaching a fifth employment placement. One guy I called seemed really interested in me, but told me he wouldn't really have any opportunities until September – the start of my second year of the course. For so many reasons by this point, I couldn't wait that long, and I pleaded with the guy to take me on there and then. I even told him that I'd work for free for the first three weeks as a trial, so that I could prove to him how indispensable I would be to his company. Even though he already had an apprentice at the time – funnily enough a lad from my college course – he took me on.

My new boss was the very definition of a slave driver, and even though the apprenticeship and college rules stated that I should be working for up to 40 hours per week, this guy had Adam and I doing closer to 70, and all for the same £80 per week standard apprenticeship wage we'd get elsewhere. Adam and I hated it, but for our own reasons, we put up with it.

One day, the three of us were working in a customer's house. I went to borrow a drill from Adam, who was working on something in another room. When I entered that room, my boss was in there with him, and he was yelling at Adam because he'd left a set of spanners on the customer's table. There was clearly no harm done, but our boss used it as an opportunity to scream at Adam about how worthless and thoughtless he was, and to threaten him with consequences should the customer complain about this seemingly terrible act. Adam was on his knees at the time, working on whatever it was that he was doing. At the end of his tether, he looked up at our boss and calmly retorted, *"you're pathetic"*. Our boss was stunned, I was stunned, and I think Adam may have even been a little stunned himself that the words had fallen out of his mouth. There wasn't too much time to dwell, however, because within seconds, our loving boss had punched Adam square in the face! Adam fell from his knees to his elbows, but got up quickly and ran crying from the room in shock. My boss turned to me and barked at me to get on with my work. I was shaking but I followed the order. Nothing more got said, but I couldn't think of anything else for the rest of that day.

I knew there was no way Adam was ever coming back to work, and so I dreaded the coming months. Having Adam with me was the only thing keeping me sane in working for this lunatic. I had to start thinking strategically though, and it didn't take me long to work out how to gain some positives. Ever the entrepreneur, I had spotted an opportunity to capitalise. The next morning, prior to getting in the van with my boss, I told him we both knew that I'd have to take on the work of two people in Adam's absence, so with that in mind, he'd need to pay me double the wages. Unsurprisingly, my boss just shouted at me to shut up and get in the van. I refused and once again stated my offer. My boss gave me a resounding *"no"* so I began to walk away. He then got out of the van and called after me, reluctantly agreeing to my terms. £160 a week was mine. You could argue I'd have more work to do, but I had been working every available hour anyway, so doubted I'd notice the difference.

My glee from my pitch and reward was to be short lived, however. Adam had reported the assault to the college, so unsurprisingly, they called me straight away to get me out of there. They told me I'd be welcome to carry on working for this guy if I wanted to, but the apprenticeship and their involvement as the qualification provider would be null and void. I had to leave.

If they hadn't said it already, my friends and family by this point were all telling me that I was either jinxed owing to all that I'd gone through with this apprenticeship, or that I should just face facts that perhaps the universe was trying to tell me that plumbing possibly wasn't the career for me. Any sane person would have accepted these statements, but I refused to do so. I willed and forced myself to believe it was all just part of the particular journey I was on. I would keep going. Back to the Yellow Pages it was.

Just two days later, Darren, my first boss, called me up. He was working for a new company, and they just happened to be looking for an apprentice! I couldn't believe it. I was about to enter into the second year of my apprenticeship, and here I was being presented with a great opportunity to work back with my original mentor. I jumped at the chance. I had a brilliant boss, the hours were a respectable 40 per week, and the pay was double the apprenticeship wage. I was once again employed, but for the first time in a while, I was actually happy in the job. It struck me that I'd really not even considered being happy as a part of this journey until now – I was just so focused on the outcome of completing my first qualification having thrown it away the first time.

I don't know if it was me or if it was Darren, but one of us was most certainly born under a bad sign. It was four months into the second year of my apprenticeship, and he called to tell me that Chris, the company owner, was folding the business. You'd think I'd have been angry, upset or confused. In reality, I was now just exhausted. Was this all my payback for messing up at school?

Out came the Yellow Pages, out came the CVs, and off I went on my travels to knock on doors. Through doing the latter, I came into contact with a guy I once knew through playing football. We had a quick catch up and he told me his dad had a plumbing business these days and that he could at least get me an interview. As it turned out, his dad was going on holiday that night so didn't want to see me until he returned, but I was so relentless in my approach to him that he agreed to give me ten minutes that evening before jetting off. I went to his house that evening, and his wife told me how young I looked. I played on it in the hope that it would make her and her husband see how lovely and angelic I was. The interview went well, and I walked out of that house after ten minutes with a job. It was £150 per week, which was more than generous, but the days would be longer than my previous placement and I would be out on a building site rather than with customers in houses, which I'd previously loved. I didn't mind at all though, as it would all be a learning experience, and I craved that.

I'm delighted to report that this placement, lucky number 7, lasted all the way to the end of my second year of my course, and contributed towards my qualification from my apprenticeship in 2007. Rather than rest on my laurels or stop to drink in the relief however, upon gaining my certificate I went straight to my boss and asked for a pay rise. I was 18 and qualified, and wanted the going rate of double what I'd been earning previously. My boss said no and claimed that I was only recently qualified so it didn't count for much. I knew that it *did*, and I knew what I was worth, so when we couldn't agree on a wage, I gave him my thanks but told him I was quitting. I knew I was destined for more. Was it a rational decision? I don't know, but it was a decision nonetheless.

What can I share with you to summarise all of this experience? Always have in your mind the next step or a final end point for what you are presently doing. Create opportunities, maintain the experience, and continue to grow through them. My experience throughout my apprenticeship was at times a complete disaster and I often couldn't find anyone to support my continuation along such a path, but I knew in my heart that despite the hideous things I witnessed and the staggering amount of knock-backs I'd experienced, I had to carry on. If you feel that way, too – keep going. Not many people will choose to stay on such a path, but if you believe you belong there, and you can visualise the reward at the destination - keep going. I did, and now I don't look back.

5. Crazy Cat Lady

With my Apprenticeship successfully completed, I was feeling good about life. Though I had committed a lot of time to study and train, I had also kept my hand in with my one true love of entrepreneurship, and was doing some cracking deals in buying, selling and trading things - like fake tracksuits and trainers. I was driving to Skegness Market with my mate, picking up said merchandise for £20, and selling it back home for £50 a time. It was an ongoing thrill that I would never have had elsewhere, and I knew that there was a market out there for people who wanted a blinding deal.

At this late teenage stage of my life, the ability to drive became fairly important to me, and so passing my test was something that was on my to-do list. My first car was an old VW Polo. I'd love to tell you that I'd traded it up from three BMX bikes or similar, which I would have been more than capable of doing, but on this occasion, it was actually my nan that had bought the car for me. Nan was always my biggest backer. No matter what mischief or trouble she saw me get into, I was her golden boy and

I could do no wrong. I loved chilling out at nan's house, and would even go there on the days that I'd decided I wasn't going to school. I would put on my uniform at home, go to my nan's, change into my ordinary clothes, then change back into my uniform before going home at the end of the 'school day' to see my mum. Nan knew how unhappy I was at school, and the way she saw it was that at least if I was at her house then I was safe and off the streets. Nan isn't the crazy cat lady I'm referring to in this chapter, by the way. I'll come to that.

Anyway - the Polo. It was an old banger in every sense of the phrase, but it was mine. It was an M Reg, and already had a good few years and miles on it by the time it ended up in my possession. I blew up the engine in the first month. It turns out that revving a one-litre engine relentlessly for ten minutes whilst pulling wheels spins on fields to impress your mates isn't exactly a mechanically sound way to run a motor vehicle. It was more or less just the engine that was affected, so I bought a new one for the car. I bought it with the money I'd earned from my apprenticeship.

Within days of telling my apprenticeship employer that I was quitting, as I'd mentioned in the last chapter, I saw an advert in a national newspaper. It was reaching out to people to persuade them to train as Gas Engineers, and was offering a £38k guaranteed salary in a London-based company upon successful completion of the course. I was drawn in straight away. I read the further details and saw that the course would cost any potential applicants a significant few grand to enrol, but the advert was clear to state that something called a Career Development Loan was available in most circumstances.

I didn't hesitate to enquire. I made an appointment at Barclays Bank, and was approved in a really simple and quick process for a Career Development Loan of £7k. That money would cover the cost of enrolling onto the course, and also allow me to relocate and support myself in the first instance where the college was located – a good two-hour drive away in Rotherham. With my college application successful, two weeks later, I'd be starting the course.

I have no idea why, but I called my former boss and told him what I was doing, thus giving him the option to take me back. He said no and wished me luck, which is probably a good thing because even if at that time he would have changed his mind, made me a great offer and asked me to stay, I wouldn't have accepted. I then told my mum about the plan, and she wasn't exactly delighted.

Taking out a loan (from an approved source), moving, training, and essentially starting a new career are all massive jumps to make and risks to take – especially when you're only 18 and doing things alone. You can't be afraid to make big decisions and take big actions, though. You have to measure the risk against the reward, and this option was just completely stacked in my favour in terms of what I wanted to achieve. As always, I had mum's support, even though she still had doubts.

So, I packed up my Polo with a microwave; seeing this as being essential for the move. This was my equivalent of going off to university. In a way it was the same, because I was moving away and I was embarking on qualifications whilst there. Why should there be a traditional way of doing things?

I wasn't going to turn up in Rotherham unprepared, so a week or so earlier, I'd responded to a lady who'd placed a local advert in a paper up there to state that she had a room to rent out. I wasn't fussy about details and called her to say I'd take it. When I turned up to move in, I knocked on the door of the old end of terrace property. The door was answered by an old lady with somewhat of a hunchback. She welcomed me into her home. I hate to hint towards a stereotype here, but the stench of cats was absolutely overwhelming. I counted about seven of them on the guided walk through the house, but it turns out my new landlady had around 14 or 15 felines in total. For me, I'd say that put her in the classification of Crazy Cat Lady status.

The house was oddly decorated, and I remember it being filled with Victorian apothecary bottles. Every surface was taken up with pottery artefacts and even a chamber pot or two! I wasn't one to judge, however, as this was costing me a fiver per night, and my room was actually lovely. It was clean, and the cats weren't allowed in there, so I was happy. There was already a TV in the room and there was a space for me to plug in my microwave. My landlady was a really lovely lady, and it wasn't long into my tenancy that she started making me breakfast and doing my washing as part of my stay there. She was so very kind to me and I'll never forget that.

Soon after moving in, I started on the Gas Engineering course at the college, and I began to learn an incredible amount. It was 2008 and it was at the time when the country was experiencing a big recession. As a result, many of the other students on the course were older gentlemen who had lost their jobs elsewhere in other industries - even in the capacity of managers. The course was marketed as an intensive one, but nonetheless it was open to anyone from any background or experience. Although I was ahead of most of the other students in terms of the fact that I'd already had a good backing in plumbing, I really looked up to those people who were re-training and who bought management and leadership experience with them. I think I was the youngest on the course by an easy 15 years, but I was to be spending every day with my fellow students, so I wanted to get on a good level with them all. It was a great group and friendships were formed.

A few months into the course at Met UK, which was the specialist college, my mum called to leave an urgent message for me to get home to Peterborough as soon as I could. My beloved nan had become really ill, and her weakening state meant that she only had about 48 hours to live. The college were brilliant about it all and granted me leave, so pretty soon I was making the two-hour drive to the hospital. I parked up, found the ward and headed straight to see my nan. She smiled at me and held my hand, though she was clearly weak. I like to think she was holding out for me, because it was literally minutes

61

later when she drifted into some kind of deep sleep. The morphine she had needed for pain relief took over, and then within 24 hours, she had peacefully passed. She was around 85 years old and had contracted pneumonia, so her body found it difficult to combat such a condition and she couldn't fight it. I stayed a few days with my family, then went back to Rotherham to start back up at college. I knew I had to carry on, and I wanted to. There was about a month and a half of graft left.

An essential part of the course required each student to build a portfolio of work and projects to show that we were able to learn and apply our skills off-site. I was really happy with my portfolio and knew it would be exactly what I needed to progress to the guaranteed £38k per year salaried job in London, which we'd learned was with a company called Par Gas. However, about a week before things were due to progress, the college delivered us all the news that Par Gas was no longer able to offer any of the successful students a job anymore. There was really little more than that in the way of explanation, and all we got to soften the blow was the offer of £500 reimbursement on our course fees - as if that would help us in any way! This was all too familiar territory now, and though I'd spent the previous two years either ignoring or laughing off the comments from my friends that I was cursed or just really not destined for this career path, I started to feel pangs of doubt. This had cost me money, after all. I was resilient, however, and set about of my own volition to find a company that I could work for upon my course completion. There was absolutely nothing local to either my hometown or where I found myself in Rotherham, but I found something further afield. Aged 19, my course was completed, I was a qualified Gas Engineer, and I was moving to Luton.

The job was within a sector of National Grid called OnStream, and sure enough, I would be working as a Gas Engineer for £38k per year. This was more money than anybody else I knew at the time was earning, and it was even more than the teachers earned who ran my course! I didn't exactly walk into the job, however. I had driven the Polo up to Coventry for the interview, even though the job itself was nowhere near there. I had no experience of formal interviews at this kind of level so I was excited, intrigued and a healthy amount of anxious. I looked around the waiting room of candidates, and saw that I was clearly the youngest. I still felt like a young teenager at the time, even though I was very nearly out of that entire phase.

The interview should have been at 1.30 in the afternoon. I was still in the waiting room at 7.30 in the evening. I was the last one waiting. At 7.35, the interviewers emerged from the boardroom with all of their belongings, and told me that they were out of time and that we all had to leave the venue as it was being locked up. The panel seemed a little irritated by everything, and told me they would invite me back another time for my interview, which of course was not what I wanted to hear. Additionally, they told me that they'd only call me up to firm up the invitation if they didn't recruit from the bank of candidates that they had already seen that day. This was most definitely not what I wanted or deserved to hear! I argued my case regarding the unprofessional situation I'd been placed in, and it seemed to shock my audience. I told them I wanted a five minute pitch with them – anywhere. They agreed. In that five minutes in the waiting room, I was somehow able to tell them everything that I've told you so far about elements of my journey which I felt conveyed my passion, resilience and energy. They called me the next day, and the job was mine. Looking back, I don't even think that I was in possession of all of the basic requirements for the role, but if anyone ever finds themselves in that situation, I'd tell them to go for it anyway, because you never know what someone will see in you, the way that panel seemed to see something in me.

I soon started work in my new career and almost instantly began to adapt my lifestyle. I traded the Polo for a new VW Golf and even got a van for work, though this belonged to my employer. I rented a nice flat all of my own and I got my first girlfriend. I started to book holidays and went on my first ever lads' holiday to Turkey, though I probably shouldn't write a chapter on that! I was focussed on my work though, and I continued to learn as well as to take steps to ensure I paid back the loan I had taken out to cover my initial training. I was living the dream and loving life, and that was important to me given all I'd come from and all I'd been through in my pursuit to achieve a level of education to get me this far. Girls, cars and money... what 19 year-old lad would turn all of that down?

My hedonistic days spanned across two years before I realised I was now bored in my job. I was 21, and I couldn't see a next level of career development in doing what I was doing. Essentially, I'd maxed out my qualification, and though the money was good, I don't believe that you earn money – I believe you earn *time*. With the time I had, I wanted to be happy. I asked myself if I could happily carry on doing the same thing every day in the job that I was in. The answer was that I couldn't.

I had been fortunate that although I'd had a great quality of life during those first two years in my formal career, I hadn't been excessive, so I found myself in a position with some money to spend. I'd become fixated on Australia for some reason, and loved the fact that it was so far away. I had heard that it was 'the' place to travel to/around for young people, and I'd become sold on the idea that this is what I wanted to do. Cold as it sounds, the kindest thing to do was to split up with my girlfriend, and I was straight with her about the fact that I couldn't stay in a relationship that wasn't making me the happiest I knew I could be. I sold my car and finished up the lease on my flat. I quit work, and within the notice period I bought an open ticket to Sydney, Australia. This wasn't going to be a holiday; I was going to stay out there – for a good while, at least!

I'd always advocate to anybody the option to travel if you can. I know it's not as easy for everyone as I've made it sound, but as I've mentioned before, if you weigh up the risks against rewards, and the latter comes out on top, you have to go with it if that's what you want. See the world, but if you really don't fancy doing that in the way I did, then at least please don't trap yourself into something you don't love doing. Again, I know it's not that easy for everyone and I'm not preaching, but also again – consider risks against rewards.

I was at a slight risk of over-thinking my decision to head off to Australia, which is why I think I moved so quickly on the quitting, splitting and selling. I needed to do this *now*, while I was young, though I honestly believe you can still do this whatever your age, as you can always come back. However, because I run a risk here of sounding irresponsible with my advice, I would also add that if you do plan to come back eventually, make sure you've got your education set in stone. If you come back home, and you've got nothing at all to share except tales of your travels, you will come back lost and depressed because you'll ultimately end up in a job you hate and that doesn't even pay you very well. I'd worked hard for my education (after throwing it away the first time at school, of course) so I knew I was in a good position if and when I came home.

Though I'd have made the journey to Sydney alone, my best friend Scott came along with me. We'd grown up together, and we both wanted to take this step. Upon arriving in Sydney, we booked in at our hostel around midnight. It was in the heart of the city's red light district. Everything was neon, but it felt impressive rather than tacky, and there were skyscrapers everywhere looming down. On a daily and nightly basis, the streets and the hostels were filled with happy, energetic, young people, and every one of them was always going to a party or coming back from another one. It was interactive, vibrant and fun. I loved it, and quickly formed the opinion that I couldn't believe I hadn't done this sooner.

As the point had been to travel, after the first week or so, Scott wanted to move on, but I wanted to stay put. I'd already got myself a job within two days so it made sense. The role was working in a call centre, as most travellers end up doing, and I had the pleasure of selling solar power to my customers – a fantastically easy sell in one of the hottest and sunniest places in the modern world. Scott and I had come here to experience everything together, but he wanted to be constantly on the move, and I was happy to make my way a little more slowly. So, with a firm agreement that we'd meet up in the next few months, Scott went off to Melbourne. I missed him, but I quickly became friends with the people from my hostel and from my call centre. Within days of starting in my job, I became top salesman, and I used my status to work hard and play hard. I worked for 12 hours each day, and spent the remaining 12 hours partying, with the odd sleep session thrown in to recharge.

I made some great friends from all over the world, and as we grew closer, a large group of us decided to save up some money and head off travelling together. We planned on taking part in a month-long schedule of events, which we embarked upon with glee. Long hours spent on buses took us from surfing in Byron Bay to visiting Steve Irwin's Zoo out on the Gold Coast. We enjoyed a three-day stay on a castaway style island, before bussing it across to go early-morning skydiving over the Great Barrier Reef. Every day was set aside for adventure. For a 21 year-old with a short attention span, this lifestyle was suiting me perfectly right now.

Always one to have an end goal, however, my plan at the end of my month of travelling adventures was to take up a job a Margaret River in Western Australia. A few days prior to this starting, we arrived in Cairns. I had carefully budgeted everything down to that day, knowing that even if I left Cairns with no money, the job would be starting soon after and I'd be earning again. However, we found out that the trip up to Margaret River was cancelled as there was no work remaining, and there was no refund or recompense. I had nothing. I would have to go home to the UK.

Thinking back, it was probably the right time to come home. I'd been out in Australia for five months and had a brilliant time, but I'd lived out of suitcases and didn't have any guarantee of the end goal that I'd aimed for. I hadn't really missed home but I'd missed challenging myself, and it was time to start up again. I came back on a Tuesday night, went pretty much straight out with my old mates to a local pub and I partied. My mum had missed me, but I think she was actually a little disappointed to see me back at home, as I was supposed to be away for at least a year.

I settled back at home in Peterborough and got a job with a local company called K&D Heating. I was happy to be back with friends and working again for all of two days, but then a major depression hit me. I was back in the situation I'd initially run from. All the people I'd travelled with in Australia were still out there, and as I watched them on social media it upset me.

As I tried hard to get myself back into a more positive mindset, I got settled in a new house. Despite having a home of my own, I felt like I was floating around for the next few months. I could feel that something else was around the corner, but I had no idea what it was, or where it would come from.

That's the thing about inspiration; you should always believe in it, even if you can't find it, and I think that's a good message here in detailing the end of this chapter of my life. Just as I'd been inspired by reading a random newspaper advert when I was 19, you have to know that inspiration can come in many different forms, and you just have to be open to the signs. For Christmas that year, my mum bought me the autobiography of somebody you may have heard of – Lord Alan Sugar. I was a mad Apprentice fan at the time, so I was excited to read all about him. I didn't know it at that stage, but that book would literally go on to change my life forever.

6. An Empire Is Born

You know that period between Christmas and New Year, where nobody really knows who they are or what they're doing? Yeah? Well that was definitely me in the 2011/12 annual handover. I felt lost, and was spending quite a bit of time on my own.

I used the solace to make a start on the book that mum had just bought me for Christmas – *What You See Is What You Get* – Lord Sugar's autobiography. Over that two or three week festive period, I read the whole thing cover to cover. I know everyone says stuff like this about books all the time, but I literally couldn't put it down. I hadn't read a book in about 10 years by this point, unless it was some kind of training manual that I'd needed in order serve me the purpose of helping me achieve one of my hard-earned qualifications.

Why had mum chosen to get me that particular gift that year? She knew I was a massive fan of The Apprentice, so that was a great start, but I think she also just needed some kind of stocking filler, so I don't really think there was too much of an inspired reason behind the purchase, other than the fact that the book was stacked on the end of the aisle you stand at in the supermarket when you're queuing up to pay for your shopping. Definitely an 'impulse buy' if I know my mum!

By the time we had safely entered the New Year for 2012, that book had become so much a part of my life that it had started to change my DNA. It completely felt like someone had flicked on a light switch inside of me. I'd always known I wanted to be a businessman, but until now, I'd had no idea how to seriously go about it.

Lord Sugar's book gave me confidence. He was just one man from Hackney, which was a very deprived borough of London, and he'd worked his way up from relative poverty as a young man to becoming this billionaire public figure that everyone knows today. In order to start his journey to that point, Lord Sugar had simply spotted a gap in the market for electronics and had learned to capitalise on it. He had exploited the gap by building his own computers and selling them on at cheaper prices than any of his competitors. This in itself didn't make him instantly rich, but it built his notoriety and his hunger, which then all led to the ultimate wealth and success that we know he has now. Whilst I was impressed and inspired, I wasn't in awe. Lord Sugar's journey hadn't seen him do anything incredible or spectacular in the traditional view of things. In other words, I viewed Lord Sugar's journey and success as completely achievable, albeit with a lot of hard work, dedication and resilience. I worked on the mantra, *"If he can do it, so can I*", and set about drafting my ideas for a business plan.

I'd never even seen a business plan before, never mind having ever written one, so I knew I was off to a bit of a non-starter if I wanted to approach a bank for a business loan, and of course I didn't have a clue how or where to start with the concept of approaching an independent investor. Instead, I applied for a loan from Tesco. You're right if you're thinking that supermarkets aren't usually in the business of offering business loans – they're not. What they're brilliant for, however, is providing great personal loans with competitive rates of interest to clients who demonstrate solid evidence that they can ultimately pay the loan back. My salary at that time was strong and secure, and marked me out as a good candidate. I think Tesco were charging around 6% interest at the time, whereas the banks wanted closer to 20%. Aside from the financial aspects however, the best part was that I didn't have to justify the reason or purpose for the loan to Tesco, because you generally don't with a personal loan, and you can just say it's for home improvements or something similar. Technically, it was true about what I'd said when I claimed my loan was for home improvements – it just wasn't necessarily *my* home I was talking about, but you'll see what I mean later on.

I was a strong candidate for the loan and Tesco were really efficient, so within two days I had £15k deposited into my bank account. I filled mum in on all the details and what had led me to make my decisions.

They were bold moves that I was making, and she looked concerned. I think she really regretted buying me that bloody book by this point. After talking things through with her though, I knew she'd support me.

With the money fresh in my account, I went out and bought a van. I'd work out further details later on, but I wanted to start somewhere for now. Whenever I talk to young entrepreneurs, I always tell them that you don't have to have everything all sorted right from the start, and that if you think it will work like that for you, it won't. Just like life, business doesn't operate that way. Most often, you have to build the perfection around the mistakes you will undoubtedly make along the way.

So, back to the van. It was a Ford Transit Connect and it cost me £2k. I then decided I would fill said van with a stash of tools for the trade, which cost me a further £3k. Next, I wanted to establish my business name. It's often really easy to dream up business names when you're first starting out, but I was thinking bigger picture by this point. I had an end goal for where I wanted my business to be in years to come and what the ultimate success would be, so it was already really important to me to think about how my business would be perceived on a wide-reaching scale. 'Joe's Plumbing' just wasn't going to cut it, and whilst it's a brilliant tag for a sole trader style of business, that wasn't what I wanted. I had a vision of my business being represented as a huge corporation, with massive glass-fronted offices in towns and cities, employees in high-end suits, and fleets of vans in every street in the locality. I pictured myself driving past one of my own vans on the motorway. I was thinking big. I needed to pick a name that would suit and match this vision, and that would lend itself well to a corporate identity.

I'd recently had a drink with a friend who had started up a company sourcing, selling and installing solar panels. He'd called the company 'Aurora', which he'd told me was the Latin word he'd most liked when he was internet-searching around for solar and sunlight related concepts. I loved that name - it had class. I headed straight for Google on my phone, and searched through a selection of different words and phrases that I liked relating to who I was and what I wanted my business to be. I looked at translating them into Latin and I progressed quickly to combining different pairs of words that I felt sounded impressive. It wasn't long before I stumbled upon '*impravio*', which I had found by way of searching for things like 'entrepreneur' and 'improvise' and from looking at random Latin-infused variations. Clear on the need to include what my business actually focused on as part of the name, I went for a hybrid of words and settled on 'ImpraGas'. It was born! The very sound of the word hinted at how impressive I wanted myself and my business to be. I know that a name is not the be-all end-all of a business, but I do still think it's an important concept to think through.

Before anyone else could take the name (although this was unlikely seeing as I'd made it up myself) I registered ImpraGas with all the legals and found myself an accountant. I had no idea what an accountant actually did, but I'd heard through advice when registering a company that having one was essential. To my mind, I just wanted to keep the maths simple – buy for X, sell for Y. This is how I'd always gauged my money and my finances, but I realised that there would be more to it with a professionally functioning business. Things like VAT and tax in general can appear terrifying, but this didn't put me off. I would hire an accountant just to make sure everything was spot on, but I'd take it upon myself to learn all about it and to ask questions. It's how I was in primary school, and it's how I was and still am to this day. You should always take it upon yourself to know the basics.

In order to fully throw myself into this new venture, I'd quit my job. For the sake of keeping a roof over my head at the very least, I knew I'd need to find some customers ASAP, and it struck me that I hadn't had any lined up in preparation. It occurred to me almost instantly that going round to individual customers' houses and carrying out routine plumbing jobs was *not* going to do anything to help me build my business or offer me financial fluidity. It would be just like what I'd been involved in on my apprenticeships and my training, and that wasn't why I was doing this. No, I needed a big contract that secured lots of homes in one go – a contract with a maintenance company, management company, letting agency, or anything in that field, really. I would need to find them, approach them, and convince them to give me a piece of their pie, because I knew that success with one agent could secure me literally hundreds of homes and properties in one fell swoop.

So, how would I go about all of this? I would buy a suit! That's right, I took £700 from my account and headed straight to Ted Baker (the shop, not the actual designer), and I bought my first ever suit – a pinstripe number that would be sure to impress. I appreciate that £700 is a lot of money to spend on a suit, but at that time, it was as big a part of my business plan as the van and the tools. At home, I tried on the suit. Peterborough would never have seen a plumber like me before! I looked sharp, fresh and presented a completely different face of plumbing. It was a far cry from my apprenticeship and training days, where I was constantly faced with the sight of one of my colleagues' arses hanging out. Just in case the suit wasn't enough, I'd also invested in a leather briefcase and one of those 'city gent' type umbrellas. I looked more banker than plumber, and you can make your own rhyming jokes there if you must!

I'm laughing as I recall these events, but there's a lot of seriousness to it as well. I may have looked 'different', but a true entrepreneur isn't afraid to change the perception of how things look and work – they mix it up. I didn't want to *follow* suit, so I *bought* a suit. Would it work? Time would tell.

On a sunny Monday morning at 10am in Peterborough, dressed in my suit, I walked down the high street and entered into the first estate agency I found in the town centre. Despite the sun, I still took my umbrella, and despite the fact I had nothing to put in it, I still took the briefcase. I clutched both as I looked around the shop floor. I had literally never pitched like this before. It started something like this:

"Hi, I'm Joseph, from ImpraGas - I'm sure you've heard of us! I'd like to speak with the Maintenance Manager, please!"

In being told that the Maintenance Manager was unavailable, I decided this wasn't an important factor, so I stood in the middle of the shop floor and continued to pitch anyway in front of the entire office – customers and everything. I figured someone had to listen, and if they didn't, I was going ahead with this anyway.

"We offer service, maintenance and breakdown repair for all your plumbing and heating needs. We are a 24-hour company, and we are changing the way plumbing and heating operates."

I repeated this performance around 15 times across 15 different sites in Peterborough that day. The staff and customers in each branch I visited probably wondered what the hell was I doing, and I guess a small part of me asked the same question of myself. However, I'm not in the habit of leaving a card – I leave an impression. My unwarranted pitch, combined with the fact that I was the sharpest-dressed and prepared-for-a-turn-in-the-weather man in Peterborough that day, meant I would certainly leave a mark.

For the next couple of days, I had a few small private maintenance jobs that I'd gleaned through friends and social media etc. I had nothing planned for the Friday though, so I suited back up, dropped the umbrella, toned down the tie and sharpened up my spiel. I went back into Peterborough and hit the agencies once more with the new approach; politely but assertively requesting formal meetings with key people. I ended that day having not only secured two meetings, but having had them result in contract success. One of them, I'm really proud to tell you, I'm still in a great relationship with, and I'd like to take this moment to thank the very wonderful Annette, the Maintenance Manager at Woodcock Holmes. Without that 'lift' she gave me that day, ImpraGas could very well have gone a different way. My contract with Annette's agency meant that I'd just won the opportunity to service 400 properties, and my meeting with the fantastic Naveed at Peterborough Homeland meant I could add another 200 to that total that day.

What inspired me to go back into the town centre that day following the events of the previous Monday? I was prepared for the fact I'd face rejection in business, but it was my mission not to give up on something until I got that definite "*no*" – or worse. I appreciate that the Monday episode would have de-motivated a lot of people, and to some extent it did with me, too, but you have to carry on and you have to fight against any possibility of rejection.

That night, I processed the enormity of what had just happened. I'd promised a lot, and now I was one man, with one van, and 600 properties. Could I do this? What's more, could I do this at any point in the 24 hour call-out I'd promised? The excitement and pride outweighed these negative thoughts, and though the adrenaline was fierce, I eventually got to sleep. Very early the next morning, I woke up to the notification on my phone of 30 jobs from my new contracts. This was real, and whilst it was overwhelming if I dwelled too long on it, I knew full well that this was a license to print money, and that each one of those jobs was a golden ticket for ImpraGas. I got straight out of bed, and by 7am I was starting work. I only finished at 11pm that night, but I'd smashed all 30 jobs; toilets, boilers... the lot. Whilst getting into bed, I checked my emails and saw notifications for close to another 30 jobs. This was insane, but in the best possible way. I was knackered, but I'd earned my own money, and at 22 years old, this was great motivation, and I had the energy to come through this.

Regardless of my actual or imagined energy levels, I knew that if I was going to continue getting this kind of call out on jobs, I'd need help, so by the end of my first week, I'd contacted Peterborough Regional College, where I'd trained for my own apprenticeship, and I took on an apprentice of my very own. The boy in question was a lad I knew from my local area, so I'd called the college about getting him registered to follow the same training path that I had. As well as being financially unviable, employing a qualified plumber wouldn't have been a right fit at the time. I needed someone to be another pair of hands, and an apprentice would be perfect for that supporting role. Plus, paying apprenticeship rates was much more straightforward and economically friendly for the business. Though apprentices can work long hours and long days for very little money, with the right mentoring, they can learn so much along the way. I wanted to teach my apprentice the skills he would need for the role, and I wanted to mentor him through anything else he may need me for – business related or not. With the right people in the lead roles, apprenticeships are invaluable. I loved mentoring my apprentice, and it felt so good to be giving back. There was something beautiful about the process, and the position I'd now found myself in to help out some kid who could have easily been in the same position I was in less than 10 years earlier. My apprentice stayed with me for three years in order to go through his full course. He worked long shifts, and he did us both proud. He was instrumental in helping me deliver what I'd promised, and that's what makes you really stand out. I knew I could - and would - dominate in this industry, at least on a local level for now. I was no standard tradesman.

Within weeks I'd secured contracts with another two estate agencies, subsequently handing me another 800 or so properties. Having an apprentice was fantastic in terms of the helping hands, but by now I needed to take on an actual qualified plumber. Remember Nathan, the lad who my school had initially sent to Peterborough Regional College with me when I was a teenager? Well, seeing as he wasn't as 'bad' as me, he went the distance on that initial course, and went on via his own pathway to qualify as a plumber. We'd stayed in touch, so I called him on the off-chance he needed a job or indeed wanted to work for me, and he signed up to ImpraGas the next day.

The move to employ Nathan was a really positive one, and our good work and reputation secured us more contracts. We were winning, and ImpraGas soon took on a third employee in the shape of Monty, who was around 20 years my senior. It was strange being the boss of someone older than me, but the relationship worked and we both got a lot out of it. We worked hard to gain each other's respect and it felt good to do this. I was so ambitious by this point and really wanted to grow, but whilst the additional employees secured us the opportunity of more work, I of course needed to shell out money for things like vehicles, tools and insurance etc for both Nathan and Monty. I also needed to make sure that they both had work available to them – not just to make it viable for me to employ and pay them, but to keep them focused on being an active part of ImpraGas. I'd met Monty through a mutual friend, and he agreed to come on board even though at the time all I could afford in the way of a vehicle for him to actually do his work was a £200 Peugeot Partner. It had no power steering and boasted two slow punctures on the front tyres, and I think Monty had to pump them up daily. I made him a promise though that in 12 months time I would get him a top van, and I meant it.

Within our first year, ImpraGas had got itself an actual office, which was in reality a disused storeroom above Woodcock's estate agency. I'm not joking when I tell you that upon moving up there for the first time, we were faced with wall to wall shit – old tables, broken chairs and random office equipment. It was perfect. On the Saturday after agreeing to take the room, the whole ImpraGas team came together to clear the place out, making good use of some of the better condition old furniture to make up for the fact we couldn't afford any new stuff. There's something about your own four walls that really makes you feel like it's a real business, and so for me, this was all coming together.

Not long after moving into the space, we realised that we needed someone in that office full time to get us organised to take a lot of the admin away from me. Her name was Debra, and she was – and still to this day is – a diamond. Debra was the sister of the owner at a company I'd briefly worked for and I'd heard she was available for work these days. Debra had always been so organised, and I knew that we got on, so she would be perfect to literally run things from my mind; calling, booking, emailing, resourcing, pricing, invoicing... the list would never end, but I knew she was the only person who could do this and I needed to have her on board. I couldn't promise her instant glamour or mega amounts of money, but I told her she would have full control of the office. Despite being twenty years older and more experienced than me, for some reason she chose to believe in me. Debra transformed how we operated. It was like ImpraGas Version 2.0. Having a new face around the place was also a nice boost for the team. Everything was starting to look and sound so much more efficient and professional, and ImpraGas continued to grow.

During those formative years of ImpraGas, I had become a ghost to my family and friends. The party lifestyle of my travelling days was a distant memory, as I realised that having your own business meant that you invest *everything* into it, and there's little such thing as 'time away'. I actually feel sick when I think about the hours, day and nights I put in to ImpraGas in those early years, but I can't be anything other than proud of myself and thankful for where it was taking me. I was seeing developments so it was worth the sacrifices; the relationships, the social life, the time and ability to eat properly. I ate one meal a day, and this was usually from a microwave. Despite how sad it sounds, I loved it.

Though it looked and seemed like everything was progressing in the right direction, a closer look at our accounts showed that ImpraGas was barely breaking even. Our overheads were wiping out much of our good work, even though our reputation was untouchable. Despite the good name, however, I was personally making less money now than I did as a sole trader. We were beginning to experience curveballs, like vans breaking down and things like that. It was frustrating, inconvenient and costly, but I was learning that this was all part of business and I learned that this was why so many small businesses struggled with expansion. You learn how to keep driving through it all though; once the vans are fixed, obviously.

7. An Apprentice Once More

By 2015, ImpraGas had a portfolio of 2,500 homes and properties on our service books, and things seemed to be going really well. Every week I would make some kind of mistake, but every day I was learning. Despite my commitment to improving, I found myself desperately seeking mentorship. I also needed investment in order to 'look' more the part. Our service was well recognised and shone brightly in the industry, but I wanted our equipment to match this level of professionalism. I wanted to be the whole package of a professional outfit, and I wanted people to know my name. I longed to put myself out there in the wider world, but I didn't have a clue where to go. I felt lost again.

I remember a particularly long day in January. I left work feeling deflated. I went home to an empty and quiet house, and I did not feel in a positive place at all. I sat in the dark and reached for my phone, searching for some kind of escapism. After around five minutes of the obligatory scrolling through Facebook, I hit upon a post from a page I followed. It was the Public Figure page belonging to Lord Sugar – though I'm *fairly* sure it's not him who runs it. The post was a last call for any final applicants wanting to apply for the 2015 series of The Apprentice. It was my eureka moment, just like when I'd seen that advert at the back of the newspaper I'd read when I'd finished my apprenticeship and decided to move to Rotherham. I lit up. I thought about how far Lord Sugar's book had brought me, and how ultimately it had now steered me to his Facebook page telling me I had just hours left to apply for his show.

Upon pressing 'send' on my meticulously put-together application, I knew I'd won.

I was excited about the possibilities of getting a call from The BBC, but I had a lot of work on with ImpraGas, so I needed to focus. About two weeks later, on a Friday night after a busy working week, I started watching a classic film from the 80s – 'Wall Street'. For those of you who aren't familiar with it, the film focuses on New York's famous Wall Street district, which is one of the most powerful financial centres in the world. The film follows the story of a young upstart who wants to be like his older mentor; determined to grow up to have all the riches and successes that *he* has. I drew parallels with this dynamic in my own life, and pondered my need for a mentor of my own. I was actually watching the film on my phone rather than on TV, and about half way through, I paused in order to check on any emails that may have come through for work. After getting up to date, I absent-mindedly began scrolling back through my inbox. I don't know what I was looking for, or if I was looking for anything at all, but I found something. Unopened and dated one week prior, there it was - an unread email from the BBC. I had no idea why I'd not seen this message and so a range of emotions ran through me. I opened it up and there was the message I'd craved – I'd been accepted to audition for the 11th series of The Apprentice! My ecstasy was short-lived, however, as I realised that the audition was less than 48 hours away! I have no idea how I missed that email, but all I can ever be grateful for is the fact that I did at least find it in time – just. I started running around the house, scrambling to get a good suit together ready for the next few days. This was it.

The first auditions were taking place near the BT Tower in London, so I made my way to Goodge Street Station on the Underground. When the Tower came into view, so did the sight of what seemed like several thousand people, all in suits, queuing outside to get in. As I walked towards and past the hoards, I began to scan my possible 'competition'. I didn't have long, however, until the doors were opened and we were all filtered into a massive room to 'wait it out'. Everybody sat in silence, with only the screech of chair legs from people nervously shifting in their seats providing any kind of soundtrack to the situation. No doubt we were all thinking the same things, and all contemplating what might happen next. This could really be my big break - whatever it was that was going to come at me. Eventually, somebody who

I presume was involved with the show walked into the room and read out a list of people to go with her. This happened every twenty minutes or so from then on, although I lost track of time. During that crossover, most of the people from the prior cohort would be ushered back into the main waiting hall and then shown out of the building. The others had been 'kept', it seemed, and presumably taken through to a new room - and the next round. After what felt like hours, my name was called.

Whatever was in that next room, I was ready. I had made sure I had a good piece ready should they ask me who I was, but you could see almost immediately the people who just were not prepared for that eventuality at all, and those who perhaps *were* prepared but just choked under the pressure. Standard responses from my competitors were pretty much along the lines of, *"Hi, I'm David, I'm an accountant, I'm 32 years old, I like cricket...."* I'm sorry, but it was dull. I was about to liven things up for everybody though, and trust me when I say that nobody was prepared for what was going to come out of my mouth during my time to shine. I put myself out there with a loud and engaging voice, complete with over-emphasised hand gestures, and exploded into a pitch. Boom, here I am!

"My name's Joey Valente, and I'm the Godfather of Business. I'm here to make you an offer you can't refuse!"

That was pretty much the start of it, and it didn't get too toned down from there, if I'm honest. I seriously believed I was the definition of success right there and then, and in my allocated time I made sure that everyone else knew that was the case, too.

By process of elimination that I wasn't ushered back out of the door that I'd been brought in through, I figured that when the crew split the group into two and began to direct us onwards, I was through to the next round. It was quite a symbolic progression, because in order to go to the next room, we had to go up in an elevator.

As the day went on, there were a number of rooms to pass through and tasks to complete in each one. Each room held a different task that was designed to let each applicant showcase their credibility as a business person – and prove they could do so whilst coming across in an entertaining way on TV in the process. I think the fourth room was my favourite room, although unfortunately I can't tell you exactly what we were asked to do in there – trade secrets! All I will say is that it was intense, and although I'd never been in that exact type of scenario before, I had *certainly* been under pressure before, and that was exactly what was being tested right now. I could do this. I had a feeling about who I believed would do well in this room from the newly formed groups that had come together. Much like I'd always looked to my Uncle Tim as someone who had a presence in the way he walked, talked and held himself, I was seeing similar people here now who knew how to carry themselves. They say never judge a book by its cover, but there's also a lot to be said for making a correlation between how someone carries themselves and how they will act or interact socially and professionally. Even their face shows if they've got what it takes – it's in their eyes.

On task completion, we were all ushered out of the same door together and wished a safe journey home. The producers literally gave nothing away regarding if we'd been successful in any way or if we'd ever hear anything again. It was around 8pm, and though I was tired, I was absolutely buzzing from the day's events. The anticipation, the competition, the pressure... I'd loved every minute of it.

As always, ImpraGas had to be my focus, and so once back in Peterborough it was back to work as usual. It was a good few weeks before I heard from the BBC production crew that I was being invited back to compete in a further audition. This time, the numbers were significantly lower, and only a room full of people joined me at the audition site. It was crazy to think how far everyone had come, especially as the rumours were doing the rounds that upwards of 50,000 people had initially applied.

As the day kicked off, the whole group was presented with two tasks that required us to line up in some kind of order in relation to set criteria that we believed to be true about ourselves. On both occasions I strode straight to the front of the line, fully expecting that there would be a power struggle. This was very literally the case, as I found myself embroiled in a minor pushing and shoving showdown with a female contender. It was absolutely crazy, but it was the pushers and shovers who were being watched, because as we all know, they're the ones who make the best TV viewing. Anyone who positioned themselves anywhere other than the front of the line in terms of being 'the best' just wasn't going to get picked, and I couldn't understand why people didn't 'get' that. The lady in question whispered to me in the scuffle that I was making a fool of myself.

*"Nobody's going to remember **you**, love"*, I retorted.

Well, *she* started it.

For the final task of the day, I ended up holding a packet of broken biscuits. Basically, using any means or skill possible, I had to make them saleable to my counterparts. I put forward the case of my biscuits serving as a *"quick and easy cheesecake base"* for any cookery fans in the room. I was quite proud of that!

My culinary prowess clearly paid off, because I soon found out that I'd been shortlisted to the last 30 applicants. We learned that from this, the producers would pick their final 18 – the cohort that would make it into 'The Boardroom' and appear as candidates on the show. My dream was becoming ever more real; so much so, that people around me were even starting to believe it now.

The next step as part of the selection process was to be sent to have an appointment with a psychiatrist. This was partly to test out if you were a nut job (I'm sorry if that's not politically correct), but mainly it was because they needed to profile us all to see who would or wouldn't hold up well in the scenario that we would be placed into if selected for the show. Essentially, you would be living in a strange house with 17 other strange people, and with each of them waiting to have their chance to take you down. Add to that the fact that all of this would be on camera. It's not like you can call your mates or your mum afterwards either for comfort or reassurance, as a requirement of the show is that you're completely cut off from everybody, and you're not even permitted to have your own phone. I was confident that even surrounded by all those egos, and the pressure of the whole concept in itself, I would be just fine. I could deal with whatever was thrown at me.

Although I was 100% confident that I would make it through, it was still immensely nerve-wracking waiting for that phone call to put me out of my misery. When the phone did eventually ring, it was at 8.45pm one night whilst I was out driving my van on a job somewhere. The number was withheld, but I just *knew* it was the producers. Sure enough, the Executive Producer of the show was on the other end of the phone, and she was passing me her congratulations. I drove straight to my mum's. She was over the moon. Filming was to start almost immediately.

As you join the official process of the series start and you move into your shared house, you start to get to know your competitors. You have to remember, though, that you're not there to socialise; you're there to win, so I instantly started to weigh everyone up. I started to judge whether people belonged there or not, and for me there were a few surprises. I couldn't fully remember any of them at all from the intensive process that we'd all just been a part of over the previous weeks. I'm not saying none of them stood out, I'm just saying that during that time I had to keep all of the focus on me and how *I* could stand out.

Just prior to moving 'on set', I had a massive decision to make. Part of the contract for the show is that you go away for a total of nine weeks to film, and during that time, you're only allowed to tell three people where you're going. At this time, ImpraGas had seven employees and close to 3,000 homes and properties on contract. Without me present, I felt that the company and all I had built could realistically fail. I would either have to risk losing everything ImpraGas was and ever could be in the hope that I'd win the show, or stay with my company and miss out on the biggest opportunity of my life. I was confident I could win the show, but I had built ImpraGas from scratch and been there 24/7 through the highs and lows of the last three years of solid graft. I was genuinely torn.

One of the people I decided to tell about the possible Apprentice venture was Debra. I told her that I could only see myself going on to the show if she could agree to step up and take full control of the business in my complete absence. Debra was only contracted to work for ImpraGas three days per week, even though I knew she took work home to get extra stuff done for me. She was hard working and she was loyal, and I knew that this was a massive ask of someone who already did so much. Although in many ways Debra ran things at the company anyway, she wasn't ultimately accountable. If she agreed to take on this mantle for me, everything would be on her shoulders. It was a massive responsibility, but there was no obligation and I'd made it clear that I could offer her no immediate reward. What I did do, though, was promise her that I would win. She nonchalantly told me that she *knew* that I would, and she agreed to run the business for me. Everything about Debra's response filled me with joy and with confidence, and I will never be able to repay her for that, though I still hold the promise to her that when I'm financially set for life, she will be, too.

With Debra on board, we hatched a plan. I was due on a train to London to start filming on Monday 26th April, 2015. So, on the Sunday evening, I sent a text or email to everyone I knew, including my employees and my customers, to say that unfortunately a family member had been taken ill over in Italy, and I would need to travel with no idea when I could return. I added to the tale that the relative in question lived on a remote goat farm and so it would be unlikely that I'd have any communication signal. It was a little ridiculous and stereotypical, I guess, but it did the trick.

Arriving at Euston station the next day, I was picked up by a member of the production company in a chauffeur-driven Mercedes with blacked-out windows. When I arrived at the infamous Boardroom, a row of 18 Mercs were present in total – one for each of the candidates. It was exuberant madness, and all added to the fact that I had no idea what was coming. Camera and sound crews were everywhere, and they swarmed to fit us all with microphones. We were about to meet Lord Sugar.

As we all waited in silence in the reception area that you will have seen so many times on TV when you've watched the show, you could hear Lord Sugar through those famous glass doors. Sat in front of us was the receptionist. I'd only ever seen her hands and the back of her head on TV, but here she was now with a face and everything! This was strange. I was 'in' the TV! Her phone rang and you could hear Lord Sugar's voice through the receiver. *"Lord Sugar will see you now"*, came the instruction from the receptionist; the one I think we'd all anticipated. I shot up and was first through those glass doors. There he was in front of me – my idol. He looked me up and down, and continued in that judgement will all of the candidates, sizing us all up by the way we presented that morning and what he was reading aloud about us based on our initial applications. He kept referring to me as *"Valentino"*, and at one point I remember him looking me dead in the eyes and saying in that gravelly cockney accent of his, *"I'm gunna remember you"*. I would make sure that he did.

Soon we were sent off in groups in those famous blacked-out people carriers you see on the show each and every week. We were driven in convoy to a £9million five-storey Georgian townhouse in Holborn, London.

Whilst I couldn't believe this was going to be my home for the next nine weeks or so, I made a mental note to myself that one day, I would *own* a house like this. We all had a quick look around the house and dropped our bags in rooms, but then it was straight on with business as the crew split us into two teams and told us to pick names. Naturally, all of this was filmed. The crew are constantly on site with you, so it always makes me think about how much was filmed that never got to air. What the cameras typically picked up in this case was everyone trying to make an impression and everyone trying their best to be heard and to lead.

After a long day, we all headed to bed. I'm a really light sleeper so it was difficult sharing a room with three or four others. It was tough for me to switch off, but I drifted off eventually. I needn't have bothered, as at 1am, the door flew open, the lights went on, and in barged the production team. The phone was ringing and we were told someone would need to answer it. The call was from Lord Sugar, and his instruction was that we had an hour to be up, alert and out the house. That was the timeframe and there was no arguing. I was half asleep and in my pants, but I was determined to be ready and to look fresh amid the chaos that ensued.

Within 90 minutes, we were all gathered at London's famous Billingsgate Fish Market at the iconic Canary Wharf. The task? Make fishcakes, or similar, to sell to wealthy bankers that lunchtime. You literally don't get much more input than that. Within minutes, we were kitted out in gloves, overcoats and hairnets, and discussing the manufacturing, marketing and selling of Nicoise salads and fishcakes, all set against the backdrop of the hustle and bustle of the vibrant early morning market. I loved it. I had no intention of putting myself forward as Project Manager for this task, as I'll be the first to admit I don't cook, but April put herself forward and I admired that as it took balls, being the first task. I would support her, as I believe that a good leader knows when to step back.

I took it upon myself in the group to negotiate on the ingredients for the creations we'd be making later that day. Despite other team members trying to get in on my deals, I ended up negotiating and securing a cracking deal on cod. Strong and assertive was the way to do this. Within hours, our team of nine were in our kitchens for the morning. They were massive sterile-looking commercial chef kitchens, and it was quite intimidating. We were joined by a top chef, but she was there for safety, not support. We were on our own. You have to remember that while all of this is going on, you've got either Karren Brady or Claude Littner as Lord Sugar's aides glaring at you throughout to add to the intensity and pressure, so mistakes would always likely be made. We managed to get through the manufacturing stage eventually before heading out in our sub-teams to sell. My station was at Moorgate, and we were selling lunchtime fishcakes for £4 apiece and charging £9 for a salad. It sounds expensive – especially if like me you aren't from London – but my sales pitch was based on the fact that I was telling these wealthy bankers passing by that they'd be paying four times as much if they dined on the same quality produce in a nearby restaurant. It worked, and we sold out.

There was no time to feel happy or hopeful though, because we were quickly transported back to the Boardroom we'd been summoned to on our first day. The task was over, but the trial was just beginning. They kept us all in that reception waiting room for hours, and we were told to sit in silence, because undoubtedly this builds tension, and even more undoubtedly this makes for brilliant television. Those Boardroom scenes are shown as ten or fifteen minute interludes on TV. In reality, you're in there for a good three or four hours until Lord Sugar utters that most fateful of phrases – *"You're fired"*. Win or lose today, I wasn't going home first.

As it turns out, our team lost, and Lord Sugar pulled us all apart for it. In the end, as most things do in business, it all comes down to numbers, and as ours were crunched, it didn't make for pleasant listening. Actually, that's not entirely true, because it was brought up in discussion that I had single-handedly sold £130 of fishcakes to our customers, which was no bad thing for a rookie lunchtime haul. That gave me a little bit of a boost, in both knowing that April couldn't justify bringing me back into that Boardroom later on, and in making me stomach whatever it was I'd have to consume in the famous cafe in Acton that the losing team infamously gets banished to each week. I sat in misery but relative peace in the cafe, and watched as our 'team' turned on each other like a pack of wolves descending on prey. I didn't need to contribute as it was clear that Dan was the weakest in the competition, sadly, and I wasn't about to get involved when I really didn't have to. I watched with some genuine sympathy though as people sensed his weakness and then zoned in on it. The attitude was laughable really, but we were all here to win, so ruthlessness would always prevail.

Without going into the detail now that I'll give you regarding future tasks detailed further in this book, April took her choice of two team 'mates' into the Boardroom for final judgement, and Dan was ultimately fired. You're not actually allowed to 'task talk' in the house prior to a decision being made, unless the crew instruct you to, as this allows for more genuine on-screen reactions. There was so much fakery there, though. Ideally, for the sake of taking out the competition, you didn't want *any* of the three summoned candidates to walk back into that house to see another week, but when the lucky two who had indeed survived the Boardroom would come in through that door, you'd see so many hugs, kisses, and fake delight. I stayed out of it all, and merely scratched a name off the list.

8. Bring On The Tasks

As far as my limited Boardroom experience was going so far, I was learning quickly that the worst thing you could do in front of Lord Sugar was to keep talking. In attempting to defend any mistakes or short-comings, people were talking themselves into graves, and so I was thankful that I'd picked up early doors on the fact that I could tell from his face when Lord Sugar had heard enough and when it was therefore time to just shut up. My philosophy was always that it would be too easy to escalate things into a bitch fight by 'doing down' everything that someone else was doing, in order to draw attention away from anything that could potentially have been my own fault, so I vowed that I would always stick with concentrating on myself and selling the reasons as to why I was credible. I always believe this is the best way to catch and retain someone's attention - stick to what you've done right and not what someone else has done wrong. Keep focused and always show contribution, commitment to further improvement, and admittance when you're wrong. Lord Sugar above all people appreciates this in business; just be honest and own up when you can. Admit you've messed up and vow you won't do it again. How can anyone fault that logic?

I would be strong enough to know, however, that if someone made a clear point of attacking me in or out of that Boardroom, I'd destroy them.

So, Task 2. There were 17 candidates left in Lord Sugar's search for his new business partner, and I was fired up. Lord Sugar himself split the teams into men versus women. The task was to market a new shampoo from scratch. The men were to create a product for men, and vice versa with the women's team. The task required both teams to carry out market research, create a digital billboard, 'make' the product, and market it. The billboard task was mine, as allocated by Richard as the Project Manager. I booked a model from an agency near to the Maida Vale studio we were recording at, who we would film using the 'shampoo'. In real life, our product was hand soap from the gents' toilets, mixed up with water to create the closest thing we could get to a luxurious lather.

I presented the model at the studio, and asked him to take his shirt off to add a bit of glamour as well as to add to the reality of him being in a shower. Before this could go ahead though, we had to get written permission for using water in any form at the studio, in order to comply with health and safety. After getting permission, I made our model stand in a bin, which would of course be out of shot but would hopefully catch the bulk of the water that I would be pouring on top of him from a watering can, from my precarious position perched on Gary's shoulders to give me enough height. Off camera, it of course looked ridiculous, but on camera, the effect actually looked amazing – in my head, at least. The resulting production was proudly displayed in black and white on a digital billboard in Victoria Station in London. It looked brilliant, and combined with everything else put together by our team, our little masterpiece gave us a win in the Boardroom. The production team even commented behind the scenes that it was actually one of the best productions of an advert that they'd seen on The Apprentice to date.

Task 3. We were driven in convoy to the beautiful White Cliffs of Dover. It was nice to be out of London for a little while. Once at the Cliffs, Lord Sugar tasked the two teams with locating and purchasing a list of items at the best possible prices. I think this tends to be one of the most popular Apprentice tasks for viewers, and I was certainly looking forward to it as a candidate. The idea was that the teams should come back with the most items possible from the list, having spent the least amount of money. There would be fines applied to the team if an item purchased was incorrect, and fines added if the item wasn't sourced at all. This task was absolutely made for me, and I desperately wanted to be Project Manager. Scott also wanted the role, but ultimately the team chose me, and this may have been down to the fact that I was gaining a reputation as someone who could get things done quickly. Just what the task needed.

We needed to split our team into sub-teams, with half staying in England, and the other half journeying on the ferry across to France – Boulogne if I remember correctly. I felt like I should lead by being the first person to volunteer to travel. Any of the information we were given regarding the destination in France and the task from that point onwards was understandably, if not unhelpfully, written in French. The locations we would be visiting would be villages rather than tourist centres, so we needed someone on that sub-team who could speak French. Richard told us he spoke the language well, but once across the Channel, this turned out to be utter rubbish. Sam had an A-Level in French, so we figured he would be our best shot at conversation if not negotiation. Richard clearly wanted to be in charge within this sub-team, but I knew that if things heated up between us as a result, I would be ready to put him in his place for the sake of keeping this mammoth and potentially tricky task on track.

Amongst the items we needed to source on our side of the English Channel was a Louis Philippe mirror, a set of crystal champagne flutes, and a specific make and weight of cheese. Sam was great in navigating the French version of the Yellow Pages, and so after two hours of driving around rural France and checking in with the sub-team back over in England, we found we had already accumulated eight of the items on the list in total from both sides of the water. We were to hit a wall, though. Ridiculous as it sounds, buying the cheese was made more difficult than it needed to be, owing to the fact that Richard's compulsion to control the situation saw him haggling with the shop assistant over the equivalent of 20p. You need to know when to leave a situation – business or not - and so after a short while I had to take Richard outside of the shop to give him a bit of a dressing down. I know it ended up on camera, but it was important to me that our conversation wasn't in front of his peers or our 'customer' at this stage. It should have been a bigger dressing down, however, as we later found out that Richard had actually negotiated a price for the cheese that was *higher* than the one it was originally on sale for!

Pretty soon, our sub-team only had the mirror, the champagne flutes and a length of lace left to find, and we had the added pressure of Lord Sugar's aid, Claude, observing our every move by this point. As luck would have it, we actually spotted an antique shop across the road from the cheese shop, and we saw by peeking through the window that it sold mirrors and champagne flutes! This would have been perfect, had the shop not displayed a sign on the door to say it would be closed for the best part of the afternoon. The rest of the team wanted to move on to save time and track the items down elsewhere, but I wanted to wait it out for the shop to re-open, being absolutely convinced that if we could just get inside, we would definitely find what we were after. This turned out to be the right call, because although we had to wait for a painstaking hour, the owner eventually turned up. We took the champagne flutes at a great price there and then, and whilst the owner didn't stock the mirror we needed, he directed us to one of his other shops which did. It was a massive stroke of luck and we were on a roll, though we knew that time was ticking on, and that if we didn't get back to the ferry in time after collecting the mirror then we'd be fined somewhere in the region of 250 Euros as a part of the task conditions, and this would undo all of the great work we'd just done. Communication with the sub-team back in England assured us that they had done a good job with only one item missing from their haul at this stage. This heartened me, but it also spurred me on to want the full amount from *our* allocation. We had one item left to go for ourselves, in the form of a material known as Leavers Lace. To go for it now was to risk missing the ferry, but I just felt like we had to try. For the second time that day, my hunch paid off, and I was doubly happy that I had done the negotiating on the price of the lace myself, but I was fully aware that nothing is fool-proof and it could have so easily turned into the biggest mistake of the task.

Our team had a good chance of winning this task, but we were all too tired to get excited. The ferry was delayed, and so after eventually getting back to the house in London at 5am, sleep wasn't really an option as we needed to be back in the Boardroom by 9am. This relentless way of operating was typical throughout the series process, and it was designed that way to truly test us. We had long hours of work with no breaks or fixed meal times, and times when we were left completely bored and with no option to even talk to each other in order for the production crew to build suspense. Sleep, in any form, was a bonus. I completely understand why the crew operated things this way, and though it was tough, I agreed with it. *I* would emerge strong and the weak would be exposed. An example of that came in the Boardroom later that morning, when all of my team said I'd been a good Project Manager, except for Richard, who was quick to put forward alternative and highly negative thoughts about my leadership. I tore into him, but really my point was proven when it emerged that our team had won, so I must have done something right.

Task 4. At this point, I knew I had some good stuff behind me. I reflected on everything I had done so far and took care to analyse positive patterns so that I could replicate them. I also made sure that I was always prepared to answer the question, should Lord Sugar ever ask me, *"Why should I keep you?"* Though I was feeling good, each of the tasks were so different and varied that I knew I couldn't take my foot off the gas. One wrong move on that show and you're in that famous firing line. The positives kept coming though, for now, and during Task 4's challenge to sell pet toys and accessories at the EXCEL exhibition space at London's Docklands, our team, Project Managed by David, pulled off another good win.

Task 5. This task saw us meet Lord Sugar in the main hall of a massive library in the centre of London.

The task was to write and promote a children's book. Despite having already taken on the role in recent tasks, I put myself forward as Project Manager, as I reckoned I'd have a pretty good imagination to lead this one, but Charleine was equally as passionate, and the fact that she had two kids herself meant that she was the logical choice when the team voted on it. It was set to be a really nice task, and I relished the opportunity to sell the dream of the book we would create.

In the early stages of coming up with concepts, I presented the idea for a character called Bizzie the Bumble Bee, and suggested that his story could follow his quest for honey. It followed the successful theme of the popular children's book, The Very Hungry Caterpillar, and for me, following a successful concept or theme and replicating it will always be a success in any business task. The book would largely be a picture book but would also be educational, therefore opening the product up to a wider market for when we were ready to pitch – in theory, at least.

The book looked great and was well-written, but we pitched it to Waterstones and it was unsuccessful. We had a similar lack of success at the smaller independent bookshops we pitched to, whereby we sold copies, but the figures were nothing near substantial enough to be happy about. Our final pitch took us to the Rainforest Cafe in London's Leicester Square, and they were so impressed with the book that they bought every single copy. Another win for our team when back in the

Boardroom with Lord Sugar, though I still to this day don't know if he ever read the book...

Task 6. This became popularly known as The Handyman Task, where each team would pitch for business to work in people's houses or shops, carrying out any maintenance work they needed doing. This should have been perfect for me to lead on given my background, but Lord Sugar picked the Project Managers this time around, and for our team he picked Elle. It was clear he wanted to see how I would deal with the allocation, but of course he will also have wanted to test out Elle, seeing as she was a former manager of 21 staff in a construction company. I accepted the decision and got on with it, and you absolutely have to do this in business, because not everything will go either your way or the way you expect it to. As a team player, I would support Elle as best as I could, and would lead wherever and whenever she needed me to. My background and experience meant I could go about such leadership with authority and support, and the team responded really well to this. Mergim, however, was a disaster for the team. He was such a great guy in general and was so full of energy and humour, and the editing during this task certainly made for great viewing, but in terms of helping his team with the task, he was an absolute liability. He was literally wrecking people's homes and shops. He was hammering in screws, painting over important signs, and telling customers that they had problems with the angles of their walls rather than realising that it was his measurements that were completely off. Despite all of this, our team completed all of our work, but we knew it would be a tough task to walk away as winners owing to the refunds we would have to give to the customers where Mergim had messed things up.

As soon as Elle was asked to present her initial thoughts about her team's performance whilst in the Boardroom later that day, she was quick to state that without me, the team wouldn't have got anywhere at all. This was massive praise for me, but it also showed a huge strength in Elle, who of course would have to shoulder a lot of responsibility for task failure, should it likely come to it, in her role as Project Manager. Karren, Lord Sugar's aide, was quick to jump in on Elle's statement, and reiterated to Lord Sugar that the team would have had no chance of being successful at all if it hadn't have been for my direction. Lord Sugar seemed a little thrown to hear such positives, but his response was to announce that he'd heard such good things about me during this task, that he was going to make me immune from being fired if our team lost. This had never happened in any of the previous ten series of the show, and the shock within the Boardroom was palpable. I felt amazing but not exactly relieved, because I knew that even without immunity, there was no legitimate reason for me to be fired that day. I was just buzzing off the fact that something so new and shocking on the show was happening – and it was happening to me.

Having said all of this, I still really wanted my team to win, so I was genuinely gutted when we lost. It came down to money, which it always does. Another shocker on the task was the fact that instead of three people going into that Boardroom and only two surviving it to see another task, Lord Sugar unceremoniously fired all three candidates. It was shocking at the time and so I can only imagine how it came across to avid viewers of the show when the episode ultimately aired. There were only two people left on our team now, including me, of course. The other team, back at the house, did the usual routine of pretending they gave a crap. The triple firing had massive impact though, understandably. Things were getting interesting and the process was speeding up. Three more down. I loved it.

Task 7 was another trip away from London for the newly shaken-up and reshuffled teams; this time, up the M6 to Manchester. It was a retail-based task, so Gary put himself forward to project manage owing to his background working for Tesco. Everyone backed him, and as someone who I definitely called a friend by this point, I was really keen for him to shine. The task required us to pick a load of products from a warehouse list to sell in pop-up discount shops in Manchester City Centre – both in one of the main shopping arcades and out in the street. We could negotiate on prices for purchasing stock at the warehouses, as the point was to see who had the most money at the end of all the buying and selling. It was a really enjoyable day, even though it was fairly bizarre picking up and peddling loads of random stuff like electric fans, paddling pools and cuddly toys.

Once again, my sub-team had Claude watching over us. It was pressure, but it was a good kind of pressure. Manchester City Centre was heaving in the sunshine, and the commotion we were causing out on the street - and the camera crew that were following us - meant that we drew a hell of a lot of attention. We'd opted mainly for kids' stuff to sell, and the toys and entertainment bits we had on offer were selling ridiculously fast. I remember one guy nearly passing by but then doubling-back to buy a paddling pool, and then I wouldn't let him leave until he took a cuddly toy as well, seeing as he'd happened to mention in our interaction that his 8 year-old brother was having a birthday party soon. I told him that if I wasn't selling the stuff I'd be buying it, and there was probably an element of truth in that, given the buzz of the atmosphere that day. There were so many people clamouring around our pop-up shop that it was difficult to process everything, but we sold out of stock and this happened seriously quickly. As Lord Sugar always says, product selection is everything. The other sub-team, overseen by Gary, had done equally well inside Manchester's famous Arndale Shopping Centre, and I wasn't surprised.

Lord Sugar wouldn't have been happy if we'd simply have sold out of stock and then called it a day. It was important that we kept working until we could make the most amount of profit available, so this meant that our team were keen to risk a mad dash back to the warehouse just prior to closing in order to pick up more stock. We re-stocked on the items that had been the most popular, and picked up some additional impulse buys whilst we were at it – stuff we knew people would succumb to grabbing whilst shopping, like cheap but nice-smelling candles, body butters and Haribo sweets.

On the second day, within the busy Arndale Centre, our Project Manager came into his own in telling us all about the *"customer journey"*. Basically, this meant putting the cheap and cheerful impulse buys at the front of the shop so that people would see them upon passing and entry, and again on exit, and so be more inclined to buy them. It's known in retail as the Halo Effect, and it worked.

Our whole team were in our element by this stage, to the point where three of us would set upon any one customer nearing the shop. It could have put people off, but in reality it worked really well, as we had some real bargains on offer, and we were selling out yet again. We couldn't take the money quickly enough, but I can't help thinking that the cameras helped the situation, whereby people wanted to be a part of what was going on. Around two hours prior to closing, with the shop still buzzing, Gary made a tough but well thought-out decision to re-stock, and sent half of us back to the warehouse to pick out more of the stock that had been selling so well. With the stuff that wasn't really shifting, Gary simply clumped it all together with more attractive products and marked them up as 'Manager's Specials'. The whole thing was orchestrated with precision. We absolutely smashed it.

The drive back down to London was as least four hours, and though spirits were sky high in our team, we were, as always, banned from task-talking. The intensity and excitement made for a great Boardroom experience with Lord Sugar, however...

"I hear you've been selling candles and body butters" he announced to our team as we took our seats. *"Sounds like a night in with Valentino, here!"* he added whilst looking at me with the closest thing I could place to affection from the business mogul. We all laughed, as we sometimes did in that Boardroom, but let me tell you that just as soon as he could make us laugh, Lord Sugar could always make us stop. In a more serious tone after his comment to me, he gave Gary a lot of well-deserved credit, and this was supported by everyone else in the team. We'd won easily, but there were feelings of awkwardness too, when we sat there to witness how quickly and how badly the other team fell apart in the face of their loss. It became clear to me that it wasn't always all about money in this process; a lot of success would be built at least in part on the relationships established within a solid team.

Our team right now was feeling great, and our win saw us being treated to a VIP tour around The Shard; London's tallest building. Looking out over all those iconic buildings and structures in the nation's capital, drinking champagne as the sun went down... I really thought I'd made it. Having said that, looking out over all that money and opportunity... I just couldn't relax or fully enjoy it. I didn't just want the view – I wanted the reality. At that moment, I felt that any minute spent daydreaming was a minute wasted; taking me away from working towards achieving my next big goal of becoming Lord Sugar's business partner. Bring on the final tasks!

9. The Road To The Final Five

Task 8 eventually presented itself, and it hit me just how close I had come to winning this contest, and earning an otherwise unattainable business partnership in the process.

The task was a million miles away from my Shard celebrations, and saw our team instructed to plan a children's party for a group of 8 year-olds. Despite his proof of solid project management in this process from the previous task, Lord Sugar insisted that Gary was put forward once again as Project Manager. Could he continue to ride the high? Could he replicate his success *outside* of his comfort zone? I believed that the answer to both of these questions was *'yes',* and I had faith in Gary whatever the task. I still to this day hold Gary in the highest regard both personally and professionally. On those 'down' days at the house, you would get to see who you got on with in a normal non-business context, and Gary was one of those people. The only thing I didn't like about him was that he snored, and so I would often have to slap him awake for disturbing my light sleeping patterns, but that's another story.

My main role in the children's party task was fairly low-key, but it ended up being incredibly significant. In a nutshell, so to speak, I'd helped Charleine sort the birthday cake for the birthday boy, and had purchased Nutella for the chore, despite *knowing* that the birthday boy's mother was allergic to nuts to such an extent that she couldn't even be in the same room as such a product. Just to make the culinary calamities even worse that day, I took ownership of the barbeque element of the party, and although I still stand by the fact that I like my sausages well done, everyone else saw them as burnt, and as a result, the parents refused to pay for the catering elements of the entire celebration. These disasters, combined with a massive cock-up involving iron-on transfers for t-shirts, meant that we lost the task spectacularly, and I was brought back into the Boardroom in the firing line as a result of my 'contributions'.

Although Gary and I were friends, we were both business people, and if either of us ever needed to hold the other one accountable, we would do it. Although he probably knew I wouldn't go down without a fight, Gary made a good call in bringing me in – but I was ready. Ultimately, the domestic ironing duties bestowed on David saw him take the bullet for the task, and though there was an element of relief, I was a little bit gutted for David because his part of the task with t-shirt printing did not in any way look simple. Let's face it; we were all in this process to show that we were business people – not cooks or maids. I'll always remember David desperately trying to 'save' the party by singing to the kids, despite the fact that we had no music. It was dreadful, but fair play to him for trying.

It's fair to say that during that Boardroom experience, Lord Sugar absolutely flew at me in anger. It was probably the first time he'd had to do this, and the first time where I did indeed need to shoulder some blame. On TV, you see that section of the show with the unlucky trio lasting for around ten or fifteen minutes. In reality, it's actually about three hours, and it is as exhausting as it is savage. On TV, the audience will take a thrill from Lord Sugar giving people a dressing down and from seeing the candidates doing enough to make themselves look foolish. It's therefore fair to say then, that you feel utterly worthless when you come out. Low as I felt at this time, I knew it was all part of the test, and in a weird way I got a buzz from it, as it was a real challenge. I actually saw the benefit of being dragged into that Boardroom, as it was a golden opportunity to really show Lord Sugar in close quarters just what I was made of. It's more 'one on one' in there, and a chance to show who you are and what you can do. I was determined to make the most of a bad situation.

On that particular occasion, there were four of us in the firing line as opposed to the usual three. This was not because Lord Sugar was really mad at the whole team, which he was, but because when he'd hinted that Charleine would be 'let-off' so to speak, she stood up to leave before he'd even finished talking. This visibly riled

Lord Sugar, and he shouted at her to sit back down – where he then insisted she stayed.

Task 9. The remaining eight candidates were gathered together one morning at the South Bank Tower in London, where we were instructed to suit up in construction gear and meet with Lord Sugar in a huge construction cage outside of the building. The wind was howling, but we managed to take on board the instruction that our task was to sell property. I had a real interest in this, so despite feeling a little self-conscious dressed in a high-vis vest and hard-hat, I was up for being Project Manager.

In my team, I had the joy of working with Selina, who by this point had become a pretty strong figure in the competition. By 'strong', I mean she was difficult to deal with. Although we hadn't worked directly together a lot, Selina and I had never really seen eye to eye, and with fewer people in the teams at this stage, I knew I'd have to watch her closely. In working together, the task required us to convince developers to sell their properties to us for us to then sell them on to clients. The team with the most commission on sales would win the task. I wanted to go straight in for the really high-end developers as big ticket targets, despite not really understanding their properties. I mis-read a lot of the dealings I had in this arena and showed that I was clearly too focused on the money. I had overlooked, somehow, that it was – and always is – of vital importance to understand your product, believe in it, be passionate about it, and sell the dream as well as the item. I really didn't do that on the first day of this task and it was a massive fault, but an even bigger learning opportunity. I remember one of the developers in question criticising my performance in the task at the time. He also used it as an opportunity to comment on the way I looked; singling out my snazzy braces in the first instance. He told me to seriously look at my own outfit, and proceeded to tell me I looked like a second-hand car salesman. I was naturally upset, but tried not to take it personally, as it was stuff that I could change if I wanted to.

When I was next alone I had a good look in the mirror, and took everything on board that had been said to me that day. I looked at my now trademark moustache, and at my haircut, which was shaved close on the sides. I wasn't ready to completely make myself over, but I wanted to show the developer – and anyone else who held his view – that I could take feedback on board and act upon it. So, the next day on the task when we met with him again, I had replicated the developer's suit choice that I had seen him wear – same style, same tones, no braces. That morning up at his property, he looked me up and down, but this time he just smiled at me.

Just one sale of one of this developer's 'Manhattan Roof Garden' properties was worth close to a million, so the commission on obtaining and selling one would be massive. Selina knew this too, of course, and there was very quickly a dogfight between us as to who made the sales. Fighting with her was unprofessional, but in this instance I felt as though the only option was to fight fire with fire.

Our team generally wasn't performing well in this task, but things changed when we met with a potential buyer in the form of a young, suave-looking guy from Chelsea, who clearly had a bit of cash. Something told me I could connect with him, and that if I didn't convince him to buy from me then I deserved to be fired that day as Project Manager. I could see very early on into the meeting though that Selina's attitude and approach was really putting this guy off doing business with us. He clearly wanted to buy, but he wanted and needed the right deal, and I was the man to pitch it to him. Boom – a three quarters of a million pound apartment – sold. I cannot express the relief I felt at that time. I felt powerful and like my true self again, and even though I'd found out that we'd lost the sale of a huge Canary Wharf property to the other team, I knew I'd personally done something fairly significant to redeem myself and at least put me ahead of Selina in the safety stakes.

In the Boardroom, it turned out that the Canary Wharf deal had clinched the win for the other team. Almost instantly, Lord Sugar beat me down about my money-grabbing attitude and lack of attention to detail on the first day of the task. I knew this was coming and so I could at least be accepting of it, but I took it as an opportunity to tell Lord Sugar that I had purely wanted to show him how good I could be at making money, but that owing to my failures I would also use it as an opportunity to show him I could learn and take on board any feedback – using the interaction with the developer as an example of my willingness to improve. Lord Sugar seemed fairly satisfied with how I'd presented myself and proceeded to move on to someone else.

Owing to the loss, our team was sent to that depressing looking cafe in Acton again, and I hated that I'd already seen the inside of that place. I didn't get much time to dwell on my cup of lukewarm builder's tea before the place descended in to chaos, as Selina and Charleine began ripping into each other. I couldn't have both of these people back in the Boardroom with me, as all hell would break loose and there was a risk Lord Sugar just wouldn't tolerate us anymore and would fire all three of us. As Project Manager, I needed to be tactical in my choices as to who to bring back with me into the Boardroom to face the firing line. I chose Selina, owing to the fact that I knew I'd performed better than her should things go head to head - and the fact that I just really wanted shot of her. I also took in Gary, because I knew he'd have my back and also put forward a strong case for staying should things turn nasty with Lord Sugar. I got my wish, and Selina was fired.

Meanwhile, on the winning team, there was to be a big upset. Scott, a candidate I had both liked and seen as a fairly close contender for winning the whole thing since the start, announced in the Boardroom upon being handed the win that he was leaving the process. I don't know exactly what it was that prompted him, but it was a massive shock and you could tell that Lord Sugar was disappointed to see him go. I was shocked and disappointed myself, but in snapping my head back into the game, I was a little bit pleased as well, owing to another rival being taken out of the competition. A successful team player and member of a winning team walking out of the process voluntarily... it was another Apprentice first, and it made for real excitement both in the house and on the viewers' TV screens.

Task 10. Imagine my delight when it was another culinary-based task. Gary, Charleine and I were teamed together one last time, and the task for the teams was to design, produce and sell a new healthy snack. We chose to go with a new energy bar as our product. The idea of health food was a little lost on me, and so I found the concept of ingredients and recipes all a bit alien. Charleine took this element on, thank god, and I went with the design aspects of the task. As it turns out, the whole bloody thing was awful – the product and the design. Our energy bar was less a mouth-watering morsel and more a bag of birdseed. Both teams had to pitch to Asda, Tesco and Holland & Barrett, and one of my roles was to gather market research out on the streets of London prior to doing this. Understandably, nobody had anything good to say about our product, and so I had to pretty ·much lie during the pitches. Luckily, I don't think the buyers heard much of what I was saying over the sound of birdseed scattering across the floor as they opened up their bars. We sold absolutely nothing, and our only saving grace throughout any of it was that, somehow, the other team did even worse with their greased-up vegetable crisps. When all of this got dissected in the Boardroom later that day, Gary and I could not stop laughing at how ludicrous everything had been. Lord Sugar soon gave us the 'look', however, to remind us where we were.

As our team had somehow won, I had automatically secured my place in the 'Final Five'. As it turned out, with Lord Sugar summing up the day's 'winners', I was the first to be put through into that most coveted of cohorts. Joining me would be Richard, Vana, Charleine, and last but not least, Gary.

At this point in the tale, let's journey back to the moustache. It's one of the first things people remember about me when my name comes up in reference to The Apprentice, so I'm aware of how significant it was, at least for fans of the show. I had a certain 'look' which I'd already toned down somewhat in Task 9. It was fair to say that the process of being on that show had changed me, and was continuing to do so. I wanted to do something momentous to show Lord Sugar that this really was happening and that I was taking things on board and improving as a person, a professional, and a potential business partner. I'm not giving anyone any groundbreaking advice here when I say that people can and will judge you on how you look. Your response to this is that you can be thick-skinned, arrogant or just plain individual, or you can look deeper and see whether or not there may be something you're putting out there that is in fact holding you back. I wanted, needed and deserved credibility, and if I had to play a certain game in order to get those things then so be it. I shaved off the moustache, and I made sure that the camera crew were there to film me doing it. This was the new and improved Joseph Valente.

I'd watched the famous 'Final Five' interview episodes of The Apprentice so many times on TV, but nothing prepared me for actually being a part of it, because I'd never really been part of an interview process quite like this in the past. I lacked the corporate experience that the others had no doubt at least familiarised themselves with at some point in their careers. All I could do was to stand by who I was when faced with my interviewers, and be ready to back up everything I said – as well as everything I'd claimed in my initial application and business plan several months previously.

The interviews for the Final Five took place in a London skyscraper affectionately known as the Cheesegrater. Iconic people in iconic buildings in an iconic city. This was it.

My first interview was with Mike Soutar; sharp, serious and Scottish. He held in his hands a copy of Lord Sugar's autobiography, *What You See Is What You Get*, and spent the majority of our interview questioning me about the very book that I'd claimed in my application was my inspiration for business and catalyst for success. I'd be lying if I said I hadn't seen this coming, but regardless of that preparation, the level of questioning was intense – especially seeing as I was rather put on the spot with the questions. It had been a good while since I'd read that book, but I knew that I had fully devoured every word at the time. Mike fired questions at me regarding age milestones in Lord Sugar's business career, and quizzed me on products and lines he was involved with. He asked me who Lord Sugar's first employee was, and probed me to find out if I knew what his first branded product on the market was. Incidentally, it was a lighter with AMS written on it. I knew the answers to all of the questions that kept coming, and I could tell that Mike, as well as all of the crew capturing this for the TV, were in disbelief. Given the pressure of the situation, I'd surprised even myself, but I think it had always been clear from that I was no bull-shitter.

When I reconvened with the other candidates in the waiting area, everyone shared war stories about how brutal their first interview was. I stayed quiet, relishing the fact that proving my credibility had made my first interview really quite enjoyable. I kept that to myself though, as firstly, I didn't want to come across as 'that guy', and secondly, I still had three more interviewers to face.

Next up to greet me was Claudine Collins. She was absolutely lovely with me really, to the point where someone has since created a meme of me and her, where I am regarded as having romanced her. Her line of questioning focused mainly on my image, so we had a lot to talk about.

After Claudine came Claude, who of course I'd had some experience of dealing with during the process this far in his role as one of Lord Sugar's aides. I was worried about this one because Claude wasn't just basing his lines of questioning on what I'd written down months earlier in my application – he would be basing them on everything he had physically witnessed me say and do to this point. I have to be fair to Claude though and say that, although on TV you see him as being fairly savage, he was actually also a good advisor and an aide to the candidates as well as to Lord Sugar. This came across in the interview stage as well, and he was considerably constructively critical about my business plan in a way that made me look at my initial thoughts with much needed objectivity. Claude praised me for how he'd seen me grow and change throughout my time as a candidate, but he was encouraging of me to tweak my business plan. This ended up being music to my ears, because I'd made some changes to it early on that I didn't actually like, but I'd done it because I thought it would appeal more to Lord Sugar. I was more than happy to change things back. It doesn't matter how good the business plan is if the person is wrong, so I was happy at this stage that I seemed to be credible in both senses.

My final interview was with a lovely lady named Linda Plant. Linda spent some time reiterating what the other interviewers had been through with me, just to test me out, I think. She asked me why I wanted a penthouse as one of my goals. *"Don't **you** want a penthouse?"* I asked her in return. She agreed with me, as no doubt she already had the penthouse, the car, the money... most people in Lord Sugar's business circles almost certainly do. I had stated either in my application or at some point during the process that I viewed Hugh Heffner as one of the most successful people in the world and someone I aspired to be like, which naturally opened itself up to questioning and criticism. I stood by my point though; the man had taken the adult entertainment industry by storm and subsequently spent his days in a luxury mansion surrounded by beautiful young women in bikinis. What single 25 year old male wouldn't be envious of that?

It's worth pointing out that, when you're not in one of your four interviews on that day, you are sat around for literally hours in that waiting room. I think the longest break I had between interviews was close to four hours. Again, this is by design, and it's set to test you. It was probably one of the most stressful days of my working life, and it was all being strung out to create drama and tension for the cameras. It can make you quite paranoid, really. I remained fairly confident with my performance despite all my fellow candidates continuing to state how they'd struggled. I stayed quiet, as I had done on any of those rare permitted task-talks in the house. If there wasn't anything to say, I wouldn't say it. I prefer to listen to people, anyway. I like learning from them.

Without a doubt, the worst thing for the candidates but the absolute best thing for the TV viewers, is where the production crew prove they really do their research to dig up anything they can find in your past that could serve to discredit you in some way. It's far too entertaining for them not to do. For me, something that was 'dug up' was a rating on a tradesmen's review website, where they had somehow found a rating from my mum – despite her having a completely different surname to me. ImpraGas had installed my mum's boiler several years earlier, and she had understandably rated the service. Claims were made that I got all my friends and family to review my company for me, but I stood by the fact that we'd carried out a service for my mum as a paying customer and she therefore had the right to comment. What's more, it wasn't even *me* that installed it for her and she'd named one of my colleagues in the review instead! Good service is good service, and deserves to be praised. And there was me worrying that they'd pick out or pick up on a *bad* review...

We all journeyed back to the house very late that night. It had been a long day, and tomorrow couldn't come soon enough for me. I needed to know if I'd made it through to the end. Exhausted as I was, I couldn't sleep, and instead spent the night pacing around, and reliving every good and positive thing I could think of that had happened to me since first entering that house and this process. I would use those stories if I needed to tomorrow, and I would prove how I had grown, learned and progressed. I went up to the rooftop terrace on my own, as I had done on so many nights at that house, and I looked out over the city skyline. *"You're the winner, Joe"*, I stated to myself. I truly believed it, too.

The next morning, we watched the famous panel of four filter into the Boardroom to feed back to Lord Sugar. *"You lot had better have sold me well, you bastards"*, I thought to myself with a giggle. Well, they must have done, because I was officially announced as the first to go through to The Apprentice Final. All that was left now was to see who my ultimate competition would be.

I witnessed the demise of three of my rivals over the next few minutes and hours. Richard wasn't straight enough down the line in answering simple questions and Lord Sugar became frustrated with him... Gone. Charleine was clearly a credible option for Lord Sugar but he just couldn't see scalability in her business plan... Gone. Gary... well, he will be the first to admit that his business plan just wasn't very good. It was something to do with a disco party, which I think he laughs about quite a lot now... Gone. The remaining candidate was Vana; smart, well brought-up, ambitious. She was the right choice. She offered a product different to anything else in Lord Sugar's portfolio, and both she and the plan were of intrigue.

I didn't believe she was as good as me, though, and I hadn't come all this way to lose.

10. Crowned The King

With emotions running high and a sense of things not quite sinking in for us both yet, Vana and I went back to the house. We had been granted two days off from the process to collect our thoughts and think about refreshing ourselves for the final task. I was so unbelievably wired about everything that it never really hit me how strange it was with just the two of us rattling around in that massive Holborn townhouse, especially considering that just weeks ago, there were 18 of us residing there. The crew was still there, of course, but there wasn't as much for them to capture given the distinct lack of arguments, personality clashes and close-quarters tension present in previous weeks.

Nice as it was to grab some rest and a sense of being left to my own devices for a couple of days, I really didn't want those two days off. I just wanted to get on – and to win. When the Final came, we got the call to see Lord Sugar. We were to meet him at the Mayor's Office at City Hall – otherwise known as The Onion. The Onion was a huge building out on the Thames, and once inside it, we were taken to a massive auditorium with a spiral staircase circling the inner walls down from the different levels. We were told that we'd be coming back to this very spot in two days to present our final version business plans to an audience of 200 business experts. I knew I could pitch and present, but never in my life had I got up and delivered my spiel as part of such a large and imposing public speaking event. It dawned on me that I'd have some work to do here, but that was a good thing, as it would keep me focused, sharp and challenged; all good things any business person should always be. I was wowed by the surroundings, and vowed to myself that whatever happened, I would not be a victim of stumbling over my words or breaking down in front of the crowd, as I'd seen happen in so many Apprentice pitches and presentations of this nature in previous years on the show.

Having watched every series of The Apprentice since it first aired on the BBC in 2005, it was no surprise when we were told that our old team mates would be coming back to support us with the final task. What we *didn't* know was who those candidates would be. I could take a fair guess, however, based on who I knew would never *want* to come back or dare show their face again. I knew that there would be some good people coming back who, if I had the opportunity to choose them before Vana grabbed them, I'd be able to use as part of a fantastic team around me. Ultimately, my team was made up of Mergim, Brett, Elle, and, of course, Gary. My choices had centred on those who I knew were good people, hard workers, and those who I could really get on with and trust to just carry out whatever I needed doing. I didn't need inspiration or innovation from anyone at this time; I just needed people I could trust to get on with things and who would back me whatever happened. As individuals and as a group, I'd always got along with these people, and I knew that they wanted me – and believed in me – to win.

Owing to a number of legal factors both within and outside of the TV Show, I couldn't pitch my business plan under the name of ImpraGas, so the company name I went for in this final task was Prime Time Plumbers. We needed to design a logo to go with this name, and Elle and Mergim stepped up to design a billboard to promote the company's branding and messages. I wanted us to cover all sectors of the industry in order to appeal to a wider audience in that room of 200 business experts, so I wanted to include my planned implementations for utilising Smartphone Technology as well as promoting any standard or specialist plumbing and heating services that we could offer. In other words, I wanted to show everybody that I wasn't just about fixing toilets! I believe you should have a number of avenues you can explore in business, just to keep options open, but as I'd already discovered with my journey at ImpraGas, it also doesn't pay to be considered as a 'Jack of all trades'. I would need to make sure that I could make this clear in my presentation.

I took Gary with me to meet commercial clients in my sector, in order to gain advice and guidance about what to pitch and how to pitch it. No matter how well you're doing in business, you can always do better, and it would be arrogant to think that you can't learn something from other people who either do what you do or buy what you sell. I went one step further in the forum, and asked all of the advisors for their business cards. It was a little unexpected and unorthodox, but as long as it wasn't against any rules of the programme, I felt comfortable in doing it.

You never know when you'll need to call those people up, Joe...

Lord Sugar later referred to the proposition as me having *"more cheek than Kim Kardashian"*.

True.

Although I haven't needed to contact any of those people yet, I certainly don't rule it out. I took on board a great deal of what was shared that day, and decided that the best route to travel down was the promotion of proactive maintenance rather than reactive service. I felt empowered and I felt positive.

My relationship with my team was really strong, and I should also point out that I had a really good relationship with Vana, too, although I obviously didn't see her much during the actual task. I knew she'd do really well, and this thought was what I needed to keep me pushing myself to be the best. I needed to fully concentrate on *me* – who I was, what I do, and how I would come across. I knew that when I would see Vana again in the Boardroom, we'd both have a lot of good stuff to share, and would both have enough about us to keep things positive and amicable. Had we been the kind of people to argue every single point and turn on the other person in a heartbeat, we wouldn't have made it this far in Lord Sugar's recruitment process – great TV though it would have been.

On the second day of the task, my team needed to produce a video advert to launch a Smartphone plumbing App that I wanted to showcase. Mergim, Elle and Brett took on this project. Brett, who had always been a hard worker but a joker nonetheless, took the opportunity to suggest to the others that they have some fun with me at this tense stage of the process. The three of them called me as I was preparing my presentation, and told me that they'd messed up the video. They told me that they'd initially thought it would be a quirky idea if they'd filmed Mergim slapping Elle on the arse and calling her *"sweetheart"* in order to convey a stereotype of a plumber, but that this hadn't been received as light-heartedly as they had meant it to upon showcasing it to people. I was horrified and speechless, until of course I watched the video for myself and saw that Brett had done an amazing job in simply turning up as an engineer to fix the boiler, with not a hint of sexism or stereotyping involved. The three of them did me so proud.

All that was left to sort out was the speech! Gary stayed up with me that night finishing the presentation slides until it was cut-off time and the crew made him leave. I was then given a few further hours to make any final tweaks, maybe until 2am. This was no longer a culmination of the last nine or ten weeks; it was the coming together of the last nine or ten years.

On the day of the presentation, I woke up feeling fresh. I really felt that everything was all coming together. Gary and I took the opportunity to walk down to City Hall rather than take the cars. There was a little bit of waiting around to do once everything was kicking off, as Vana had drawn the straw to present first. Obviously we didn't see her presentation, but by the round of applause and cheering we could hear at the end of her pitch, it was clear she'd nailed it.

When it came to my turn, it transpired that I was expected to 'make an entrance', and would therefore be entering the auditorium via a door at the top of the winding staircase. What would my reception be? I was naturally a little stressed out, but soon feeling confident as my entrance was serenaded with clapping and cheering from the waiting audience below. This wave of confidence filled my body and replaced any nerves I may have had to that point. It genuinely felt like this was going to be a supportive engagement, rather than everyone waiting for their chance to see me mess up. I could see Karren and Claude, along with Lord Sugar, in the front row. They were looking up at me, and they were smiling warmly. My public speaking career was born, and I loved it.

First up, I confidently introduced myself and my company, Prime Time Plumbers. I presented for around half an hour to fill the expected allocated time, and knew that I had got all of my messages across without that post-interview feeling of beating yourself up because you've missed something. During the question and answer session, I didn't once feel tripped up or like I was being tricked, and in fact I saw the whole opportunity as a great chance to back up any claims I'd made and consolidate any proof that my business plan was the real deal and that I was the right person to drive it forward. The Q&A session was just a wonderful chance to justify everything – the plan, the last nine weeks, and the last ten years of my life. Looking back, I wouldn't have changed anything, and the only criticism I really had to face was that our team had spent too long on choosing a name for the company. I could live with that, and joked that all of the good names had already been taken.

The reception had been amazing, and I'd made sure to thank everyone for listening to me before walking off stage with my head held high. I felt amazing, and like I'd really enjoyed myself. The way I felt about my own performance was reflected in the faces and the reactions of my team mates, as they hugged me excitedly and filled me with praise. The 'panel', if that's what we can call the 200-strong congregation, had made claims I'd chosen my team mates because they were my friends rather than people who I could prove would add value. I responded with the fact that their friendship and support were exactly the ingredients I needed in order to add value to what I was doing right now. I wasn't shy in saying that this wasn't a team game anyway at this stage – this was the Joseph Valente show! I was happy to make jokes as I felt my sense of humour was a warm aspect to my personality that had served me well in the whole Apprentice process to date, but I was very careful to fully thank and praise my team mates for what they had done for me throughout. I'm still friends with all of them today, and proud to know them all as successful people.

I travelled back to the house alone. It was all out of my hands now. There was one more final Boardroom meeting with Lord Sugar - together with Vana as my rival - but I had already done everything I possibly could have done. That night, everyone had been invited back to stay at the house, and it was actually a nice feeling. Being alone with your thoughts at a time of such anticipation can be very detrimental, as it's a fine line of reflection between your lows and your highs. A lot of those candidates who had come back that night had of course been back 'at home' for a good number of weeks by this point, and so it was good to hear their stories about how things had been for them back in normality. It got me thinking about the five-minute phonecalls we had been allowed each week to contact home, and how much of a come-down there would be after those fleeting moments of hearing the voices of your loved ones. I remember the stress I went through one weekend, when instead of calling my mum or my girlfriend, I called Debra at the office. I'd always said to her at the start, *"If I ask you how things are going at Impra, just don't tell me"*. Well, Debra took that instruction on board fully and so dutifully didn't tell me when it was inevitably the first question I asked after we'd exchanged the initial pleasantries. *"I'll speak to you when you get back"*, was her reply. Oh god, what the hell did *that* mean?

After a low-key but fun night of reminiscing, I looked forward to the next morning. It would be the biggest day of my life. I relished it, but in a way it was kind of sad, knowing that I'd be journeying across London in one of those famous blacked-out Mercs for the final time, and that I'd be taking a seat in that infamous Boardroom for the final time, too. This time tomorrow night, I'd be home.

When the day came, I realised just how much I had built all of this up, and how much it clearly meant to me. I felt like I might cry. Lord Sugar was actually really nice to us. He took the opportunity to sum us up, and gave us both time to say what we needed to say. I gave him my speech, although in all honesty, I hadn't really planned it, because I just knew that the right thing would come to me on the day and in the moment. Without putting myself through the agony of watching myself back on TV to recount the pitch word for word, I recall it went something like this...

"I once read a book that changed my life. I'm now sitting in front of the author who wrote that book. I'm young, I need mentoring. If you give me that, I'll make you a million pounds within five years."

Vana had to follow with her summation, and though it was more than credible, it seemed more rehearsed and more generic, in the fact that she did what most people would do and professionally listed her key qualities. I didn't care what she said really, as I truly believed that my speech was the most heartfelt and real.

We waited in silence for a few moments as Lord Sugar took everything on board. What would he say? Who would he choose? We would find out what he would say within the next few minutes. We would only find out who he would choose in *December – six months* from this point! What do I mean? Well, the crew filmed two endings, with both Vana and I being on the receiving end of the famous *"You're Hired"* finger point. I was gutted.

In filming the version where Lord Sugar pointed that famous finger and hired *me* to be his business partner, he first told me that although I spoke a language he could understand, and that he believed I would *"go far"* under his direction, he was also clear to state that *"technology has been my best friend for a long time"*, thus alluding to the fact that Vana's dating slash gaming-based business was a better fit for him. He then threw in a curveball, however, by adding that he thought *"it's time to make new friends..."*

"Joseph, you're hired."

Six months. You only find out who won, and which version of the final scenes will air, the morning that the final episode is shown to millions of expectant viewers on the BBC, giving you a whole 12 hours head start on the general public. They wait this long because Lord Sugar and his many aides spend that six month 'break' tracking everything that you go on to do in life; albeit from a distance. They want to size you up in terms of how you react in the aftermath of the show. Do you keep your nose clean? Do you become some kind of media whore who cares more about the reality TV lifestyle than genuine business opportunity? Is there anything in that time that would highlight through due diligence that your business is in any way unsound? I could see how my age and the reputation I had gained as a bit of character within the show made me somewhat of a risk, and so Vana could have easily won with this in mind.

As I got ready to head back to reality, I had one piece of advice running through my head, and that was what Lord Sugar had said to Vana and I in private away from the cameras a few minutes earlier. He told us to keep our heads down and to stay out of nightclubs. I got the sense that, owing to our different character styles, he meant this more for me... Was this his way of telling me early on that he didn't want me to mess up because at that stage I was the winner? I'll never know.

I got in a taxi, provided by the BBC, and I began the journey home to my old life. Although it was a Sunday night and there was nothing I could really do at that time about work, I picked up my work phone and delved into a ten week mess of missed messages. I read and listened to a deluge of questions from colleagues and clients; querying where the hell I was and asking if I was ever planning on coming back to ImpraGas... All of this, and I was still bound under contract not to tell a soul where

I had been or what I'd been doing. The same went for my personal phone and my social media accounts, and it killed me that I just couldn't tell anyone at all until the series aired on the BBC later that year and it could all finally be out in the open. In a world where social media is so prevalent however, keeping quiet and resolute was anything but easy. In the tasks where we'd been out on the streets amongst the general public with the camera crew all around us, people had cottoned on to the fact that the next series of The Apprentice was being filmed, and so were photographing the scenes and posting, sharing, re-tweeting and tagging them all over the place online. Unsurprisingly, people I knew who were Apprentice fans and following the action were recognising me in full view. Nonetheless, even when faced with the most blatant visual evidence, I had no choice but to deny any involvement and move on. It was ridiculous, but due to the non-disclosure contract I was under, lying was my only option.

Before I'd gone on the show, I'd booked a holiday to Croatia. You can imagine how well that news went down with my staff and customers less than a week after getting back from my 3 month hiatus. I had to take the holiday though, and I joked with Debra that one more week wouldn't hurt. Other than my mum and my girlfriend, Debra was the key person I needed and wanted to catch up with, and it had transpired very quickly that she had done an amazing job in keeping ImpraGas going that whole time I was away. We may not have made any extra money, but that wasn't her job, and the most important thing was that we hadn't *lost* any money, employees or customers either. I will never be able to repay Debra enough for keeping things going, and for making sure that I had something to come back to – especially given the fact that I had no idea what would be happening to me or the business for another six months.

After the holiday, I got straight back to work and waited it out until October when Series 11 of The Apprentice would finally air. How would I come across on TV? Would I be fairly edited? Would it look like I deserved to win? I honestly didn't have any answers. When October came, I was of course getting a public reaction, but I still had to keep my head down. I was gutted about this because there was a lot of stuff I was invited to in the capacity of a 'reality TV star', but I knew that this wasn't the person I wanted or needed to be right now, so I shied away. The last thing I wanted to do was piss off Lord Sugar by 'playing the celebrity game' as he referred to it. Business is sustainable - fame isn't.

One morning in December, Lord Sugar called me personally to tell me I'd won. The news was massive, but the call itself was a little underwhelming. My feelings would change later that night, however, when Jack Dee, comedian and presenter of the BBC 2 Apprentice sister show, 'You're Hired' uttered those wonderful words in the minutes following the airing of The Apprentice Series 11 Final... *"Let me introduce you to the Winner, ladies and gentlemen, Joseph Valente!"* I walked onto the stage of that chat show and was met with the most wonderful cheers, and a standing ovation from my friends and family in the front row.

Flashback 10 years to when I last saw my mum crying.

Tonight, mum was crying again, but this time, her tears were those of pride and joy for the son who swore to her one decade ago, that one day, he'd make her proud of him.

11. The Billionaire And His Boardroom

I really think that I could generate a fairly profitable business if I had a quid for every time someone asks me what it was really like to meet and work with Lord Sugar. Those people have usually seen a side of him on the show and from other media representations, and are keen to know the real details. Mainly, people want to know if you really do go on to work with him after you win the show. *Is he actually your business partner? Do you really get the money? Do you even see him again?*

The answer to all of those questions is 'yes', and, once he's 'hired' you, it's like any employment or business expectation, starting with the fact that you sign your contract. The terms of the show highlight that you do indeed go 50/50 in a business partnership with Lord Sugar, and then you both proceed through all the legals before the £250k investment gets transferred into your business account; so no option for me to spend it on the penthouse I'd already bragged about in my pieces to camera on the show! In terms of your business, you can spend the money on whatever you like. Lord Sugar needs to approve any spending of course, but technically you're free to do what you want, seeing as you pretty much wrote your planned expenditure into the business plan that he hired you as a result of anyway.

Every month following your initial partnership agreement, you attend a Board Meeting that lasts for around one hour. Along with Lord Sugar, you are faced at these meetings with his Finance Director, the Assistant Finance Director, his Accountant and the Company Secretary. The quorum represents what is known as the "*crack team of elite*", although these are Lord Sugar's words, not mine.

It was different for me than it was for any of the previous Apprentice winners who had gained a business partnership with Lord Sugar, as I already had the business set up rather than having to build something purely from a plan, so I was transferring everything rather than starting from scratch. As a result, Lord Sugar's team needed to take time to learn about what I'd already built and where I already was. This took a lot of time. ImpraGas had built a small but steady success over the years since I'd started it, but it wasn't ready to go national right away, as per my business plan. There was a lot of work to do.

Although an hour a month doesn't sound like a great deal of time, it was long enough as far as I was concerned, as it was more intense and more 'real' than the Boardroom scenarios I'd been faced with previously as part of the show.

It was strange seeing and interacting with Lord Sugar off camera. Everything seemed so much more important, which of course it was. At those monthly meetings, I was heading into an actual Boardroom scenario, and although Lord Sugar was my business partner, I felt alone at best, considering the fact that he was always flanked by his established team during every session. Having said all of this, Lord Sugar's empire wasn't based in the huge offices filled with thousands of employees that I'd expected. I think only 30 or 40 people worked for him, and this number included family members, such as his sons. It was clear he liked to keep things close and controlled, which I have a lot of respect for. You walk up to the building he is based in and you see his car outside straight away, which is pretty cool. I have to say that outside of the Board Meetings, I enjoyed the environment of Lord Sugar's empire. There was no bullshit, it wasn't overly corporate, and everything was just a little unorthodox. It suited my style, and I knew where I stood.

The only downside to 'knowing your place' is when that position becomes different to what you expected it to be. I was supposed to be Lord Sugar's business partner, but it felt more like I worked *for* him – along with everyone else. I appreciate that my circumstances were a little different to those of previous winners of the show, in the fact that Lord Sugar needed to completely fund them, but with me he was using his money to actively buy in to something that was already established and already mine. I was all for advice at this stage, but in reality I was just being told what to do, and I struggled to accept that for a lot of reasons. Firstly, ImpraGas was *my* business and I'd already done a pretty good job in starting, growing and succeeding with it. Secondly, your partner shouldn't have authority over you but should be your equal, which I didn't feel was the case thanks to Lord Sugar's companions. Thirdly, I'm generally not good with being told what to do, anyway....

Things were even more difficult with Lord Sugar's 'crack team', because as well as them knowing little about the industry they were now immersed in, I got the feeling they kind of resented me a little for being a partner rather than an employee – like *they* were. It always seemed like it was 'me vs them', and that they were constantly trying to score points in front of Lord Sugar to show they were better than me. They would always raise things in meetings that I had no idea about, because I'd not even been told about them, never mind invited to discuss. It was a very confusing time. The team was undoubtedly made up of professionals though in terms of qualification, and they did try to get on board with me, but their advice was limited owing to us having completely different skill-sets and experiences relating to the industry we were focussing on. I wanted to build a national empire out of ImpraGas, but of course none of those people in the Boardroom had experience of doing that in the Plumbing and Heating industry.

I may not have been in love with the team I was meeting with each month, but I must credit them fairly and say that they hugely helped ImpraGas with all things financial and compliance, so my business was building upon a fantastic infrastructure, which is vital to any growing business, regardless of industry. I needed to use those foundations as a confidence boost and to see what I could do about the areas I lacked experience in but desperately needed – like forming a solid national growth strategy, for example.

Lord Sugar is a powerful man, and if any fans claim he wasn't trying to control things, then they would have had a different opinion if they would have seen how he reacted with other aspects of my life during our partnership. For example, if I did any interviews or talks in the media, or shared certain social media posts, he would voice an opinion about it and tell me not to do it again. I was being told off, it seemed, and I didn't like that. It irked me even more than it would have done ordinarily, because any money I was getting from such exposure either directly or indirectly, I was channelling straight back into the business, which I thought Lord Sugar would have loved given his own media career. He didn't care, though. He wanted me to focus purely on the business, and not on anything related to the social *or* media sides of things. I guess this is because he still viewed me as a slight risk owing to my age and my character. He didn't want me getting distracted or caught up in anything that wasn't pure business.

I struggled not only with the censorship, but also with the restrictions in place towards what I really wanted to do, which was to deliver talks to tell my story and to help other business people in some way. I wanted to be an inspiration if I could – especially to young people. I felt like Lord Sugar really shouldn't get to have a handle on that part of my life, but somehow he did. I thought we were in this together, but even if there was a glimmer of hope about him showing me any kind of positivity or pride, he would nevertheless always side with his team over me if they cast a different view. He's known them forever, of course, and I was the new kid.

It was a tricky first six months for all of us, and a period that saw big changes. I learned a key lesson in the fact that you don't have to stick with your first ideas or plans in business, and that you can always streamline your offer. I always thought that expansion in business meant to offer *more* things, but the opposite is in fact true. The key is to instead offer *one* thing, and make a point of doing it really well. Get yourself into a position where you can do this so well that you can also do it rapidly. You need to make yourself a literal expert in your field. This is what I learned to do with ImpraGas as the business model changed within the Sugar partnership. We looked at what we did well and what brought us big ticket value. It was clear that boiler installation was the way to go seeing as it brought bigger money and took the least amount of output. This needed to be the service on which we focused all of our resource moving forward. We were to become the 'Michelin Star' provider of boiler installation services, it seemed. In focusing on this, we'd had to terminate all of the property maintenance contracts that had been hard-won and had provided our bread and butter since day one, and so in sentimental ways it felt quite sad, but in pure business terms, it was absolutely the right thing to do.

The ultimate aim was to make ImpraGas a national company within 36 months of the partnership, and things were looking promising. No more fixing toilets on random call-outs; this was so much bigger. Lord Sugar and his team didn't actually agree with this business model at first as they felt I was rushing into it far too soon, but they knew how headstrong I was and that I do sadly stop listening to advice if I don't agree with it, and so they did what they could to support the shift. Financial-based people tend to be very conservative by the nature and accountability of their job, and there is a massive place for that approach in any business, but I don't believe you can run an empire purely on that process – you need to take risks.

Based on our original model during 2015, around about the time I was applying for the show, ImpraGas sales had totalled an impressive £350k for a relatively small business. In the first 8 months of the Lord Sugar partnership from the start of 2016, sales did indeed improve as you would expect, but it was only when I got my own way, so to speak, from August in that year, when our sales based on the new model started to rocket; taking us to an impressive £2.1million within the first 12 months of the new installation model. I knew things could go further.

In April of this year, I was starting to get really frustrated with the lack of true understanding that I needed and craved from Lord Sugar and his team of advisors. I want to be clear and state that any negative feelings were nothing personal against anybody; I just wanted to run with things and be back in charge of my own business. The partnership with Lord Sugar had lasted well over a year but, I think we both knew it had run its course. We had a conversation, and we both agreed it was the right time to split. There was no bad feeling at all and I still very much felt that although I'd perhaps shown I wasn't the right fit for the partnership anymore, Lord Sugar still regarded me with a degree of affection. I wanted to move onwards in an industry that I knew so well but that he had little interest in. You can't blame him for that – it's not all about the money, and you have to love what you do. We wanted to remain in a good relationship, though. I owe a massive amount to Lord Sugar and to what he's done for me.

It was a clean break from Lord Sugar, as neither of us want to drag things out; it's not our style, and procrastination would ultimately lead to loss of finances for both of us. He had agreed for me to buy his 50% share of ImpraGas and we shook on the deal. We remain on good terms to this day, and he's always said he'd be on the end of the phone or email if I ever needed him. On the occasions I've called up or dropped him a line, he's proved true to that word.

I had worried a little about how I was going to explain the dissolution of the partnership with Lord Sugar to my staff. There was a risk that they would worry or even panic that parting from one of the UK's biggest business moguls meant we were in trouble of some sort, but as the reality was far from that misconception, I was easily able to communicate to the team that their jobs were safe, our company was not at risk, and that things would actually be better all round now that ImpraGas was back under my full direction; I was the one who founded it, after all – and made a pretty big success of it, too.

Thinking about 'going it alone' was a little bit sad really, because this hugely impressive person had been such a massive part of my life over the years, even though I'd only physically known him for two of them. I would genuinely love to have made Lord Sugar £100million during our work together, and would have craved his contentment that he'd made the right decision in 'hiring' me. Change is good though, and you have to be confident to know when it's right to steer from the blueprint. I'd learned so much as Lord Sugar's business partner, but it was time to move on, and if I could make £100million for anyone now it would be for my ImpraGas team. Good businesses are built on great people, and ImpraGas is no exception.

I want to start 'summing up' this chapter by saying again that I have so much to thank Lord Sugar for. I learned from him in the flesh even more than I'd learned from him in his book just prior to starting up ImpraGas, and it's all of those things that inspired me to write my very own book that you are hopefully enjoying right now. Lord Sugar didn't have to pick me as his 'Apprentice' in

2015, but he did, and because of that I know such much more about opportunity and venture, and I will be forever grateful. I always knew that I would be successful, and I think that even if I hadn't won on The Apprentice or if it had never even been on my radar in the first place, good things would have happened for me in business, the way they already were doing. However, Lord Sugar had given me a platform from which to showcase my hard work and have it recognised, and you can't put a price on that kind of opportunity.

Since the decision to split from Lord Sugar and to buy out his half of ImpraGas to bring it solely back under my control, we've had our most profitable month in business and have become recognised as an award-winning boiler installation service. We're growing from strength to strength. Debra, who for so long was the 'hub' of everything we did, sadly retired in November 2016. She will forever be a great loss to the company that she essentially helped me to develop, and whilst I'm delighted for her that she's now happily retired, I will always seek ways to properly repay her.

As we move forward with ImpraGas, we are looking to launch a product called ImpraCare, which is a boiler maintenance and central heating cover package designed to rival Home Care from British Gas. You've always got to give the people options! We had got the boiler installation service so spot on, that we were able to look at what we could 'bolt on' to this service as an added extra. We are expanding into double figures of counties we operate within as we speak, and are even creeping away from the south up towards the North as part of our plan to become nationwide within the next year or so. I said earlier on in this book that one of my business visions was seeing ImpraGas vans up and down the motorway network across the country, and I have indeed now witnessed this sight. Admittedly, they're not everywhere I look, but it's getting there. I've never been more convinced that I'm on the right path for my journey at this time.

12. The Three Step Success Philosophy

Just prior to deciding to write this book, I took some time to sit back and analyse the last ten years or so of my life. Something was working for me and for the things going on in my journey, but I didn't know exactly what it was. I was accomplishing great things but I believed they were all down to more than just hard work or chance. There had to be a pattern or philosophy behind it all.

I looked through the chapters of my life, much as you are looking through the chapters of this book right now. I began to piece together everything that had ever really happened to me, and it became clear that there were very simple steps leading to each and every aspect of success or achievement in my life. When I give my talks and keynote speeches out at schools, colleges, businesses or institutions, I refer to this as my Three Step Success philosophy.

What is this philosophy? A simple pattern of *Create, Maintain, Continue to Grow...*

Step One: *Create* – Everything in life, such as relationships, businesses, projects; they all begin with opportunity, and a key part of this is knowing that you often need to work to create those opportunities for yourself rather than waiting for them to proverbially 'knock'. I always look to create opportunities for myself if they don't fall into my path, as to wait for them is a waste of time and resource. In my life I'd shown evidence of creating opportunities for myself at a very early age, for example when all of my apprenticeships fell apart and I needed to have a Plan B (through to G), and when I decided I was going to go and start a new life in Rotherham with a lovely old lady and her house full of felines...

Step Two: *Maintain* – Once you have that opportunity firmly in your grasp, be ready to put in a lot of hard work to keep the creation moving; and moving in the right direction! This maintenance may not always be exciting, but it's essential in getting the structures and foundations right for your creations to pay off. By the time I started ImpraGas, I was working 18 hours a day, sleeping at my desk at night, and sacrificing any kind of meal other than those that had been nuked in a metal box. It's kind of 'behind the scenes' stuff, but you need to be ready to do it. The same goes for relationships; if you want them to work, you need to keep doing all of the things that you were happy to do at the start, such as making quality time for each other, going out, sharing in activities... whatever it is - put the work in.

Step Three: *Continue to Grow* - The process and philosophy don't stop unless *you* do, and so you need to stay motivated. I realise that this is easier said than done, and I know from my own experience that we all lose our way at some point. I'd talked in earlier chapters about feeling lost, alone, and not knowing what it was I needed or even wanted to do next to drag myself out of a depression. Even when I'd achieved a dream role of having become Lord Sugar's business partner – a man who had been my idol for so long, and a man who had chosen out of close to 60,000 applicants to invest £250k into *my* business – I wanted the next step. I had to trust the process and just go with what I felt was right in pushing forward. Believe in the Laws of Attraction, if you can. Continued growth is your next creation and your next opportunity.

It's important to know that these three steps are very much part of a cycle, and so while you're busy continuing to grow, you should always be looking out for catching, finding or ideally creating the next opportunity. Success doesn't stop, and when you've achieved something, that's exactly the right time to plan the next achievement. Growth is opportunity. An example of following this cycle within my own life goes back to that year when I'd been expelled from school and came to the realisation that I had to do something with my life. What did I do? If you remember, I called up my friend's cousin, Darren, and I told him I'd work for free. I knew that if I put myself forward for that, then it would create me an opportunity to work and to build skills, it would teach me the value of maintaining this process towards an outcome (in my case having Darren enrol me onto an Apprenticeship at the local college), and I would continue to grow via that study pathway to take me from unpaid lackey to qualified apprentice. Nobody likes the idea of working for free, but you have to admit, it set me off on a pretty successful cycle...

I love opportunity, and I thrive on it, which is why my Three Step Success philosophy is based on it. *"Don't wait for opportunities, create them"*. It's a mantra or quote that is often a key feature within my talks, interviews and social media posts. This doesn't mean that I have always taken every opportunity in front of me or have gone out and created one at every turn. Cast your mind back a good few chapters in this book and you'll know this to be true. The chance to start my plumbing career early before being expelled from school, for example... I completely didn't take that opportunity. Why? It could have been down to my age, arrogance or inexperience, or it could have been down to the fact that it just didn't feel right for me at that time. It was the same with taking one of the coveted candidate slots on The Apprentice back in 2015. I would never have taken that wonderful opportunity if Debra wouldn't have agreed to look after the fruits of my labour, ImpraGas, during the time I would need to be away. Weigh up your choices, but remember that it's great to at least have them!

When I'm looking back on the steps I've taken and cycles I've completed in my life so far, it's never been beyond me to stop and consider how things may have turned out if I hadn't won The Apprentice back in 2015

– or even if I'd never featured on it all. I have to think about things like this, because as I've already alluded to in the previous chapter, the whole experience gave me the biggest opportunity of my life to have a platform from which to create, maintain and continue to grow in all that I was doing in business. What I'm confident of, however, is that without The Apprentice, I would have still moved forward - it just would have been at a different speed and in a different vehicle, and there's nothing wrong with that if you still end up at the destination you ultimately want to get to.

Right now, I'm still very much following and believing in the Three Step Success philosophy and continuing on the cycle. Much as from an early stage I'd aspired to go from traditional plumbing overalls into a suit and tie, I'm now wanting to move onwards, further still, from running the plumbing business as my only venture. I'm aware I sound a little bit like Lord Sugar when I say, "*plumbing has been my best friend for a long time, but it's time to make new friends*". It's true, though. I'd like to know what else is out there alongside my continued strength to strength journey with ImpraGas.

In the meantime though, I'm incredibly focussed on developing apprentices within the business. When I was myself an apprentice in the most literal sense, not the TV star capacity, I never saw my qualification as the ultimate end goal. I always knew that completion of the apprenticeship would give me a platform to jump onwards and upwards to something else. The qualification was an aim, not a destination, and I'm passionate about giving other young people the opportunity to work towards the same platforms and cycles of opportunity and success when we recruit them to ImpraGas.

I was a drop-out at school when you think about it, because I didn't take the opportunities that were put to me. It may not have been my actual decision to leave the school, but it was my action that fuelled the result. I was a drop-out before starting up on a pathway towards - and on track with - an apprenticeship, but an apprenticeship is by no means a drop-out pathway. Vocational study, even at an earlier level whilst students are still in school, can lead towards a very lucrative career if you work hard, and I want young people to see this. If you want to do well in anything, you have to work hard, and apprenticeships are no different. If I can mentor my apprentices to share this vision and work hard, then it will be an opportunity I've created, an ethos I've maintained, and a pathway that I've continued to grow for the benefit of young people who may, or may not, have been just like me at that age.

You may assume at this point that when I talk about employing apprentices, I am doing so from within a plumbing and engineering capacity. This isn't the case. Apprenticeships exist in so many different sectors and specialisms, and I've always been keen for ImpraGas to embrace this range of skills. Presently, we employ apprentices in Digital Marketing and in Business Administration as well as Plumbing and Engineering.

Perhaps I'm hoping to find the next Debra, as opposed to the next Joseph Valente!

I'm proud of all of my staff and each of my apprentices at ImpraGas and have already stated how our success in recent years has been down to them as much as to anything that my win on The Apprentice gave me. For the purposes of highlighting the importance of following the Three Step Success philosophy, however, I'm going to single out one young girl who shall remain nameless to preserve her modest approach to her work... She joined ImpraGas when she was 18. It was a time of slight uncertainty for the business, as there was some restructuring going on following my hiatus away filming with the BBC. This girl was a great appointment in an apprenticeship role as she listened to all instructions and advice and did everything she was asked to do. We talk about an entitled generation these days, and so finding someone who is willing to do seemingly meaningless, boring or repetitive administration tasks with a smile on their face is key, if not rare. It became clear very quickly, however, that my apprentice was capable of so much more than a traditional apprenticeship job specification may expect. She took charge of situations and began to take initiative to organise and lead interactions with suppliers. She created this opportunity. In maintaining this opportunity, this young girl was keen to become a public face within the ImpraGas team, and carried out lots of her work in the open within the company, as opposed to behind the scenes where we would have initially expected such an apprentice to fit more comfortably. From this maintenance of her somewhat revised remit, my apprentice continued to grow in her role, and was soon taking responsibility for orders averaging around the £2k mark due to her strong relationship with suppliers. I don't know many apprentices who would be willing, if even able, to take on such accountability.

This fantastic young girl kept the cycle going, and showed great commitment to me, to ImpraGas, and to the Three Step Success philosophy. Within a year she was qualified at Level 2 (though I ranked her a lot higher than this) and was earning double what she had been originally taking home. Two years further on, and this young former apprentice now heads up Field Operations and Engineer Logistics. Improving and impressing at ImpraGas.

If this amazing young person in question continues with her ambition and drive to create, maintain and continue to grow, I can see her building a very successful career. That's the thing about my own cycle on the philosophy – I'm keen to recognise in other people when it's time to start a new cycle elsewhere.

It's definitely time for *me* to at least begin thinking about starting a new cycle in addition to our plans to grow the opportunities at ImpraGas, that's for sure...

13. Who Is Joseph Valente?

There's no getting away from the fact that if members of the general public recognise my name, then it's very likely down to my candidacy and ultimate win on The Apprentice back in 2015. Hopefully, through reading this book, you'll have seen that there was so much more to me prior to the show even being a part of my life, and will therefore have gone on to form an opinion that makes you want to keep your eyes open for me in any new projects in the future.

I'd mentioned during the chapter about working as Lord Sugar's business partner that I got a lot of enjoyment out of delivering talks and interviews, and so I'm pleased to say that I continue to serve as a keynote speaker at many events as part of what I do in my day to day life right now away from ImpraGas. My talks are bespoke to my audience, and usually last around half an hour, so if you ever find such time spare and want to come and listen to me speak, I hope you will feel the motivation to do so.

What am I working on right now? Well, I've just launched www.JosephValente.com, and will be keeping it up to date with everything that's going on with my professional life. I'm very active on social media and so that's another outlet for me to show the world just how closely I am sticking to Chapter 12's Three Step Success philosophy!

I love ImpraGas with all my heart and soul, having already made significant progress to drive the company national 2020, one day I will l move away a little from the day to day running of the business so that I can concentrate working on the business not in it. Having some money freed up - should I seek an investor to take on some of my share - would be a nice bonus, as I believe that you need to learn to truly enjoy personal wealth if you gain it as an entrepreneur; what with the temptation nearly always being about reinvesting it straight back into your own company. As an entrepreneur, you should look to grow profits, seek further investments and scale your projects. I may indeed decide to invest into a new project entirely, providing that I believe in it, I'm passionate about it and I can 'get into bed' with the right people. Lord Sugar always told me that business is like a marriage, and you have to be with the right person if it's ever going to survive the long haul. Before I enjoy any of that wealth myself, I'll always make sure that the people who have loved and supported me on my journey are looked after financially.

Although I've not really mentioned it in this book, I'd dabbled for a while in the world of property as I was developing as a business person. This was partly because

I had an interest in the sector, which had stemmed from our maintenance contracts at ImpraGas, but mainly it was because I like to look to successful business people for ideas and influence, and a lot of them would say that there's plenty of money to be made in property. Interest + profit = a worthy business opportunity, in my opinion. One thing's for sure, if I do more fully venture down this road, I'll be taking some lessons learned from that infamous task during my time on The Apprentice; the one which saw me dress down my dress sense and power up my passion for the product as well as the money.

As you know by now, I have a passion for speaking to and developing young people – particularly through the championing of apprenticeships. I have been fortunate to speak in schools and colleges up and down the country about the matter, and have been involved in a number of apprenticeship and enterprise projects on a national scale in the role of speaker, guest judge, mentor and/or ambassador. I have truly loved every minute of these events, and so as a result, I will be launching the Joseph Valente Mentoring Academy in Janurary 2018. Whilst my focus was at first going to be with apprentices, I realise that I can always play an active part with that demographic anyway via the projects I am frequently invited to be a part of, as mentioned. Instead, my Academy will be focusing on a key demographic of adult entrepreneurs, and through my mentoring programme, I will be aiming to motivate, inspire and teach my mentees how to start their own businesses and go on to build them successfully. Entrepreneurship is certainly on the rise in today's society, but so many entrepreneurs are 'going it alone' in the truest sense, and so could therefore really benefit from mentorship. Having someone in place to support you from the start can help you hit the ground running and steer you away from pointless tasks in order to drive you towards more pressing issues that you may not have otherwise even considered. This isn't to say that my mentorship will provide wraparound care for my mentees, as I honestly believe that the best way to develop in business is by making mistakes and learning from them. The Academy will aim to promote monthly events on specialist topics and will encourage networking activities and forum opportunities for our members. New customer acquisition, raising finance, business growth... these were all challenges and areas that I had nobody to help me out with as start-up business concepts in the beginning with ImpraGas, and whilst I personally enjoyed the challenge of learning all about them for myself, I appreciate that not everybody wants or can afford to operate in that way.

My aim will be to grow The Academy over time and hopefully recruit lots of ambassadors, which I think would be particularly nice if such cohorts included previous graduates of The Academy. We will be launching things in steady stages, but you know my thoughts on always creating opportunities and what that can then lead to! One thing is certain about The Academy – I will be at the forefront of its delivery. I'm not a fan of people who put their name to something but are unable or unwilling to put their presence to it as well. I want to be there for people, and to see how this pans out for all of us.

These days, I know that my own passion for learning will never subside. I am hoping that through working with my mentees in The Academy, I too will be inspired to keep on learning, training and developing. I have two mentors of my own already, but I do believe that I will also learn from the people I intend to mentor myself. Although I already know how to run a successful business (I hope), there is a learning path that I would still like to follow, in the sense that I've always wanted to work towards a Business Degree. I like to study, and I read a lot and listen to audio books on the move as I travel around. Although I already have the fundamentals, the experience and the applied working knowledge of business, I think it's a good thing to have a formal qualification to 'back things up' should it ever be needed. It will feel more complete, at the very least. I will always stand by the fact, however, that once you've learned how to make money, there's not a great deal else that you can be taught in business. I don't know if everyone would agree with that, but it's just my view.

At times like these I think back to Lord Sugar's 'crack team'. They were so highly qualified it's untrue, but they had little experience in actual industry. This didn't matter, though, because they were there to fulfil a role that Lord Sugar wasn't necessarily qualified in himself. This is what good business people do, though – they surround themselves with people who can do what they can't.   Every good business person does this, because they are not afraid to admit that you're never going to know everything yourself.

Though I consider myself primarily as a successful business person, I guess I'll never fully shake the tag of being classed as a reality TV star, given the platform that catapulted me to where I am right now. It's a common theme these days that reality TV stars simply further their fame by jumping from one show to the next in a bid to achieve further popularity over further cohorts of fellow contestants. They are famous simply for being famous. For me, being on TV was never about popularity. If it would have been, then I possibly wouldn't have won, as there were other 'characters' in that Apprentice line-up who you could argue were highly likeable, entertaining and more made for TV – Gary, Scott, Mergim... For me though, I never entered that contest to make friends, get screen time or mess around. I entered it to learn, and ultimately to win the prize on offer from a man who, at that point, was my complete business inspiration. So, when I'm asked if I would ever do reality TV again in the future, then I'd have to say I'm not sure. There's too much about me, and I've worked too hard to make sure that people know me and my name for the right reasons. I guess you should never say never, but I'd much rather follow the TV route of having my own business show or perhaps even a chat show. I'm all about interacting with people, helping them and learning from them, so those kinds of shows really do appeal to me. I've enjoyed being a guest on other people's shows and being interviewed - especially for news broadcasts and political or educational slots. Something a little lighter to balance this out along the way might be quite nice too, though – I'm a young lad, after all, and if you work hard you should play hard, as they say. Big Brother, however? Unlikely.

I'm often asked in interviews or by the people I meet if I would ever change anything about my life, or if I would do anything differently if I had my time over again. I would. I would change how I approached my secondary education. I'd take the opportunity to learn and qualify the first time around, and I'd focus my attitude to get that right the first time, too. You can learn at any age, but that shouldn't mean that you ignore such opportunities - or even actively throw them away - the first time they are presented to you. This is why I love speaking at events where the audience is made up of schools kids and school leavers. They love the story about me being expelled, but I use it to show them that this isn't a badge of honour, and that they can get to where they want to be so much more quickly and easily if they take education – in any form – more seriously.

I tend to get a really good response when speaking at events, and I like that people want to have a conversation with me afterwards. People will usually reference their views on me from when I was on The Apprentice, and that's fine – it's where I became well-known to a wide audience, after all. I've never had anyone say anything

169

negative or offensive to me when approaching me at such events, and whilst I still stand by the fact that being on that show wasn't about being popular or winning friends, it's nice to hear you are well thought of. I was always myself on the show, and so you won't really see a difference in my personality now if you come up and meet with me after a speaking event. People's opinions of you don't define you, however, so if someone sees you in a different way to how you think you're seen or want to be seen, it doesn't matter. Everyone will always have an opinion, but if people bother to get to know you on your journey, they'll see the real you eventually. I guess this works in both directions for those who try to put on an act or a presentation in front of people. At some point in your timeline, people will see you for what you are. Hopefully, in the case of your good self, they'll respect and like what they see.

Whilst I was writing this book, I was asked if I think I'll be the next Alan Sugar. Well, I wouldn't mind being a billionaire, and I certainly like the idea of being one of the best known business moguls the UK has seen, but do I want to be the next Alan Sugar? No. This is nothing against him, it's just that I don't want to be the next *anybody* – I want to be *me*. Lord Sugar is who he is, and I don't think anyone will ever be quite like him, anyway. Likewise, if anyone ever said to me, *"I want to be the next Joseph Valente"*, I'd tell them *"No – be the next **you**!"* You can be inspired by someone else, learn from someone else, and you can certainly always learn from someone else's *mistakes*, that's for sure, but always, always, be *you*.

With that in mind, who is Joseph Valente? Well, let's start with the fact that despite my name, I've never spoken Italian in my life. I should learn, and I would like to, because what if at some point I have to go and spend nine weeks on a remote goat farm in Italy supporting an ailing relative...?

Who am I? I'm someone who's two years away from their target of being a millionaire by the time they're 30. If I make that money, then I know I'll have fulfilled my true aim of being successful, because money is just a bi-product of success in business. I don't want to be given the money, I don't want to stumble across it – I want to earn it. I want the accomplishment, the achievements and the status. For example, I love sending my mum away on holidays to treat her, more than I could ever love going on a holiday myself. I always say I'd buy a yacht if I made my first million, but even then, it's not the yacht I actually want – it's being able to tell people I *own* a yacht! Does that make sense? I would hope that people would then look at me and think, *"Bloody hell – he must be doing really well in business!"* Believe it or not, I really don't want to come across as vain, much as that last statement may contradict that thought, but those who know me well know that my view on material objects is that they're not always as good or attractive as they first seem. I've learned not to be distracted by them, and will always stay focussed on the bigger picture.

Will I ever reach the destination in that bigger picture? I doubt it. There will always be a yearning for accomplishment that will keep me pushing further, harder and higher. This will make me happy, though, and it's the buzz that keeps me alive. I find it difficult to get that same buzz from my Apprentice achievement anymore, because it's been and gone. It will only ever have a shelf-life, and now that it's over, I need the next high. It's been fun reliving it all through writing this book, but it spurs me on now to think that in the future, I may write another book about something even more exciting. I hope you'll read it.

In drawing my book to a close, I'll reiterate a point that I made right at the beginning, which alludes to the fact that there are many reasons why you, the reader, chose this book, and why I, the author, decided to write it. I wanted to create something enjoyable, and something that would entertain, inspire and inform. I think a book like this documents what can be achieved with the right vision, attitude, philosophy and willingness to put in the hard work. I am hopeful that the book has converted any cynics who may have believed that all I had about me was the fact that I was the young plumber with the moustache on The Apprentice a few years back. For me personally, though, the book is a reminder of where my life has taken me, and how my past may shape where it will take me from this point onwards...

Create, maintain... continue to grow.

I'd love you to stay in touch

www.josephvalente.com

Or follow

Twitter: @MrJosephValente

Insta: @MrJosephValente_

Facebook: Joseph Valente

Linkedin: Joseph Valente

Youtube: Joseph Valente

Thanks,

Joseph Valente

32060051R00102

Printed in Great Britain
by Amazon